The _____ ve-
loped _____ no
tourists. They are unknown even to most ____ ks.
The only people you see are the indigenous
peasants and shepherds, whose way of life has
changed little in a thousand years and whose
friendliness and hospitality more than make up
for the lack of organised facilities. Ideal country
for walking, these mountains are big enough and
rugged enough to give a real sense of adventure,
yet are relatively safe and require no special
expertise. The walking season lasts from May to
September, and even longer, depending on
altitude and latitude.

THE MOUNTAINS OF GREECE
A Walker's Guide

Mt.Olympus - looking over Zonaria. Photo: Alistair Scott

THE MOUNTAINS OF GREECE

A WALKER'S GUIDE

Tim Salmon

CICERONE PRESS
HARMONY HALL, MILNTHORPE, CUMBRIA, ENGLAND

ISBN 0 902 363 638

FOR FLORICA

Front Cover:
The ridge between Ayos Nicholas and Petrilo,
Pindos Mountains. Photo: A.Hosking

Back Cover:
Above the Agrafiotis gorge. Photo: Tim Salmon

ERRATA Misplaced Text.
The two paragraphs on P.128 and top para-
graph P.129 should go on P.133 after 2nd
para ending 'old needles'.
P.139 - The description of the walk from Ayia
Lavra to Kerasia, to the end of P.139 should
come before the Ascent of Mt. Athos, on
P.137.

CONTENTS

Part One: Introduction and Basic Information . . .   7

Mountain life / History / Fauna & Flora / Books / Addresses / Maps / Where to obtain maps / Route-finding / Sleeping & eating / Getting on with people / Weather & when to go/ What to take / Emergency services / Getting to the mountains / Using the book / Abreviations.

Part Two: Delphi to Albania...   19

Section One: Amfissa to Karpenisi via Artotina and Krikello (including ascents of Mts.Ghiona, Vardousia & Velouhi). . . .   19

Section Two: Karpenisi to Metsovo via Vrangiana, Mesohora, Haliki (including traverse of Agrafa mountains & Aspropotamos river valley)...   52

Section Three: Metsovo to Mt.Gramos (including traverse of Mts.Gamila & Smolikas)...   82

Part Three: Shorter Walks: One to Five Days...   103

Central Greece: Mts.Oiti / Parnassos / Parnitha (9 routes)...   104

Evvia: Mts.Dirfi / Ochi / Xerovouni...   125

Northern Greece: Mts.Athos / Gamila (including Vikos gorge) / Olympus / Pelion...   135

Peloponnese: Mt.Helmos / Mani / Mts.Parnona / Taygetos / Ziria...   159

Island of Samos...   168

Part Four: Glossary . . .   170

Mt Olympus - Kaki Skala: close to the summit
Photo: Alistair Scott.

PART ONE

Introduction

INTRODUCTION

Mountains cover most of Greece. Many of them are over 2000 metres in altitude. They are unexplored, undeveloped and very beautiful. Though rugged, they are surprisingly green, forested and well-watered, especially in central and northern Greece.

There are no organised facilities for the walker or indeed any kind of tourism. There are hardly any roads beyond a few dirt tracks of the second-gear variety. So the walker can enjoy a very real sense of exploring virgin territory in mountains that are not essentially difficult or dangerous. You need to be in good physical shape, certainly - there is no repairing to comfortable restaurants or hotel lounges after a hard day in the hills. But no special expertise is necessary, beyond the hill-walker's skills. The Greek mountains are walkers' mountains, and this is primarily a walker's book. There is scope for rock-climbing, but it is best to consult the Hellenic Alpine Club (see below) on this score.

Traditional mountain life

One of the most interesting features of the Greek mountains is that they are still inhabited, albeit by an ageing and dwindling population, who carry on a way of life that has remained largely unchanged for centuries. Their beautiful, decaying villages have neither electricity nor running water. Some are accessible only on foot. Many are cut off by snow in winter. Shepherds still migrate between lowlands in the winter and mountain pastures in the summer, where they live in huts of stone or branches, cooking on open fires, sleeping on beds of brash, milking by hand, making their cheese - doing the things that shepherds have done since Homer's time. Women spin, distaff in hand, as they go about their business. You still come occasionally upon some local celebration where a couple of ancients on fiddle and drum wail out the old songs of the mountains.

A little history

In the north and west you still find descendants of shepherd clans, like the Sarakatsans and Vlachs, who have preserved a separate and distinctive identity to this day. The Vlachs are particularly interesting because their language, in contrast to all the other Balkan tongues south of Roumania, is Latin-based. No one quite knows who they are or how they came to speak Latin. Nomads, with no written
8

language, they have left no records. They call themselves *'arumani'* -Romans. While they are obviously not that, the language they speak is probably not much different from that heard round shepherds' camp fires 2000 years ago.

There are villages everywhere, and you wonder why mountains that are so rugged and inaccessible should ever have been so populated. It is this very inaccessibility which provides the answer. People sought refuge in these natural fastnesses, especially from the Turks who overran and terrorised the lowlands from their capture of Constantinople in 1453 until, in the case of northern Greece, the First World War. It was the outlawed sheep-rustlers and brigands, known as *klephts*, who made their lairs in the mountains and formed what we would now call the liberation army that finally drove the Turks out and instituted the beginnings of the modern Greek state in the 1820's

During the Second World War, many Greeks again took to their mountains to form one of Europe's biggest Resistance movements. With the outbreak of civil war in 1946, for which many Greeks blame the British, a new generation of outlaws made the mountains their base. This time they were communist guerrillas, mostly veterans of the Resistance, who felt that Anglo-American domination, restoration of the monarchy and the return of the old politicians from their safe wartime haven in Egypt was not what they had fought for. It was this war which occasioned the promulgation of the Truman Doctrine and America's first attempt to stem the so-called tide of communist infiltration.

The mountain communities endured ten years of war in the 1940's, more than their frail economy could stand. Combined with the pressures of modernisation, these privations hastened their decline.

The history of the mountains is told largely in song - the stuff of legend. And that seems fitting. There is something distinctly noble, not to say heroic, about these mountains and their people.

Fauna and flora

The fauna are thin on the ground, thanks to the Greeks' love of shooting. You see surprisingly little wild life for such wild and remote terrain. The occasional fox or hare, perhaps a deer, and adder, salamander, partridge, ring-doves, tortoises, the odd eagle or griffon vulture, a number of small birds I cannot identify - not much else. If you are lucky you might see mountain goats on Mt Olympus or a wild boar in the north-west. Bear and wolf exist - the latter, apparently, in increasing numbers, but you would be extremely lucky (or unlucky) to meet either.

Flowers, on the other hand, abound. The best season for seeing them depends on altitude and latitude. Take Mt Parnassos, for instance, in the southern part of central Greece. In the first half of May you will find fritillaries, orchids, ophrys, violets, aubretia, iris, anemones, daphne oloeides up to 1200 metres or so. As you approach the melting snow patches, around 1600-1800 metres, there are crocuses, squills, corydalis solida, saxifrages and so on. Further south spring comes earlier; further north, later. Tulips, gentians, narcissus, campanulas, geraniums, aquilegias, lilies - all sorts of glorious species are to be found, over 600 of them endemics.

Books

Patrick Leigh Fermor: *Mani* (John Murray 1958) and *Roumeli* (John Murray 1966). The two best travel books about remote rural and mountain Greece.

J.K.Campbell: *Honour, Family and Patronage* (Oxford 1964). A very interesting, if slightly dry, study of the Sarakatsan shepherds in the Mt Gamila region in north-west Greece.

A.J.B.Wace and M.S.Thompson: *The Nomads of the Balkans* (Methuen 1914). A fascinating account of living among the Vlachs, but very hard to get hold of.

Juliet du Boulay: *Portrait of a Greek Mountain Village* (Oxford 1974). A detailed study based on the author's personal experience. Again, very interesting, though indigestibly academic in parts.

Arthus Foss: *Epirus* (Faber 1978). A readable, if unexciting account of the history, traditions and people of Epirus.

Kevin Andrews: *The Flight of Ikaros* (Penguin 1984). A very well written and readable account of the author's experiences wandering about southern Greece during the civil war.

C.M.Woodhouse: *The Struggle for Greece 1941-49* (Hart-Davis, McGibbon 1976). The best and most balanced account of the Resistance, with whom the author fought, and the ensuing civil war. Very expensive.

Anthony Huxley and William Taylor: *Flowers of Greece and the Aegean* (Chatto and Windus 1977). The best field guide by far.

Oleg Polunin: *Flowers of Greece and the Balkans* (Oxford 1980). Very expensive and rather bulky. Its big attraction is that it describes particularly good flower-hunting areas of the mountains in detail.

Mark Ellingham: *The Rough Guide to Greece* (RKP 1984). Much the most readable and entertaining general guide with lots of practical information.

Addresses for information

1. U.K:

National Tourist Organisation of Greece (Greek acronym, EOT), 195-197 Regent's St., London WIR 8DL (01-734-5997). They supply a free handout, detailing mountain refuges and ski facilities and not a lot else.

2. Greece:

Hellenic Alpine Club (HAC; Greek acronym, EOS), Platia Kapnikaréas 2, Athens ((01)-3231-867). There are no real benefits of membership unless you live in Greece. But you would be made very welcome, especially if you were a member of a foreign club. It could be worth checking their programme of guided walks, even if you are only visiting. Members meet informally every evening from about 8 p.m. The club is just 5 minutes walk down Ermóu Street from Sintagma, the main square of Athens - on the R by a little Byzantine church that occupies the middle of the roadway. Usually someone can be found who speaks English, French or German. You might pick up some useful information; it depends who you talk to. The club also sells sketch maps of individual mountains.

Pindos, 4a Leofóros Alexàndras, Athens ((01)-8214-971). Easy to find near the National Archaeological Museum, this is the only proper mountain equipment shop in Greece. Mihális Kótaris who runs it is also one of the most useful sources of information.

Provincial Clubs   (I have listed the ones most likely to be of use and indicated in brackets the name of any mountain mentioned here with a refuge controlled by one of them):

Aràhova (Mt Parnassós)   ((0267)-31-392)

Dráma, Efédron Axiomatikòn 21 ((0521)-23-054)

Halkída (Mt Dírfi), Tsirigóti 10 ((0221)-25.230)

Hanià, Crete: Mihelidàki 5 ((0821)-24-647)

Ioànnina (Mt Gamíla), Monaimidou 6, ((0651)-22138)

Karpenísi (Mt Velóuhi), Zinopóulou 25 ((0237)-22-394

Kalàvrita (Mt Helmós), ((0692)-22-346)

Lamía (Mts Oíti and Vardóusia), Ipsilàntou 25 ((231)-26-786)

Litòhoro (Mt Olympus), Kentrikí Platia ((0352)-21-329)

Mètsovo, Nikolàou Gàtsou 2 ((0656)-41-249)

Sparta (Mts Parnon and Tàygetos), Kentrìki Platìa ((0731)-26-574)

Thessalonìki, Kàrolou Dil 15 ((031)- 278-288)

Vòlos, Dimitriàdos 92 ((0421)-25-696)

Maps

There are no good maps available commercially. The 1:50,000 series are a closely guarded secret of the army cartography service. The largest available are the 1:200,000 series published by the National Statistical Service of Greece (NSSG), with all place names in Greek. They give a general idea of the terrain, but are neither sufficiently detailed to walk from nor absolutely accurate. Contours are at 200 metre intervals. Each sheet covers only one *nomòs* or county in detail. Despite these drawbacks they are worth carrying.

The British Ministry of Defence World 1:500,000 series give perhaps the best general idea of the terrain, and despite their smaller scale are often more accurate in marking the line of the major mule paths.

During the last war the British General Staff reproduced an earlier Greek 1:100,000 series, which, although out of date as far as roads are concerned, provide a detailed and faithful record of paths, telephone lines and other such vital route-finding clues. They are still much the best maps that any Briton is ever likely to get a sight of, and that, unfortunately, only in the British Museum map room. Worth the trouble, if you are seriously interested.

Where to obtain maps

In London, NSSG maps are on sale at: Edward Stanford, 12 Long Acre, London WC2 (01-835-1321) (also, some sheets of the Ministry of Defence World series still available); and McCarta Ltd., 122 Kings Cross Rd., London WC1 (01-278-8276).

In Athens, you have to go to the NSSG offices, in an arcade at Likòurgou 14, near Omònia Square. It is the right place, no matter how improbable it may appear!

Route-finding

In the absence of good maps, I have tried to 'talk' the walker over the routes described in this book. Do not be discouraged. It is not really that difficult to find your way. A few mountains have more or less consistently waymarked paths. Forest tracks are easy to follow. And the unmarked majority of paths are, for the most part, pretty clear. Even when not much frequented today, they have been in use for so long that they are well trodden into the ground. Signs to look for in tricky places are dollops of mule dung, scuffed stones and roots scarred by the passage of feet and hooves. With time you develop a sixth sense for the probable line of a path. Even if you do get lost, you cannot come to much harm in summer. Above the treeline, where paths are most likely to peter out, shepherds are never far away. They are always extremely friendly - they lead a lonely existence - so never hesitate to ask them for help, food, water or shelter, if you are in need.

When asking for directions, insist on being shown the footpath *(monopåtee)*. Locals take the view that no one in their right minds would walk for pleasure and that all strangers are too dumb and physically incapable to follow a path. They,therefore, show you the dirt road - *dheemòsyo,* or public road, as they call it - if there is one. When you insist on the *monopåtee,* they tell you no one goes that way any more, it is overgrown and you will get lost. I have been told that countless times. Stick to your guns. The path is always shorter and more interesting, and all the paths described here are perfectly passable. If there are any difficult bits, I have indicated them. When local people finally give in and show you the path, you can trust their directions and their estimates of distance, always given in hours - a practice I have adopted.

Sleeping and eating

Country towns generally have at least one basic hotel. Mountain villages seldom do, and they do not have any shops either. What they all have, however, is a coffee-shop-cum-general-store-cum-social centre. It is called *magazèe* in Greek. Make your way to the *magazèe* and ask for somewhere to sleep. Very often you will be put up in a deserted house or invited home. The question of payment is tricky. People can be offended if you try to pay for hospitality. The best thing is to offer to pay beforehand. That way you will find out what is expected of you. In general, if you are invited to someone's house you will not be expected to pay. The same goes for eating.

Camping is possible anywhere in the mountains and no one will object. As the land belongs to no one, there is no question of trespassing. Just be careful of sheepdogs: they are always half-starved and a piece of human thigh is as good as a mutton bone. You do not need a tent in summer; a survival bag is quite sufficient.

There are a number of mountain refuges run by the HAC. I have

13

mentioned them in the guide where appropriate. With the exception of guarded ones on Mt Olympus, they are always locked. The problems involved in obtaining and returning the keys far outweigh any benefits - again: in summer.

As for eating, there again ask at the *magazèe*. They will always fix you a meal. The fare is basic - eggs, macaroni, potatoes, tomatoes, beans. Meat and fruit are rare in the back country. The charge is usually nominal.

Food for the road can be a problem. Special backpacking products do not exist. Mainly, you have to make do with local fare: bread, cheese and olives, supplemented by endless tins of sardines or spam, which is all that is available in remote *magazyà* (plural of *magazèe*). You will however, be constantly waylaid on mountain-tops by shepherds who want to chat and feed you. Their staple is bowls of boiled sheep's milk, salted, with chunks of bread broken into it. You come to relish it in the absence of anything else!

Whenever you hit a place with a restaurant and shops, have a blow-out and stock up. Avoid things that leak and squash in rucksacks, or are dry and salty - they are horrible when you are hot and thirsty. Be careful with cheeses, especially the ubiquitous *'feta'*. The dry variety is often salty, and the more edible wet one leaks. I go for the hard *gruyère* type of cheese, called *gravyéra*, when I can get it. Taste cheeses before committing yourself. Whole salamis are good, and though they sweat they keep. Halva *(halvà)* is a good sugary energy-giver. Nuts, sultanas and dried fruit are readily available in the towns. I am a muesli addict; it is light, unmessy and quite palatable when mixed only with spring water, but unobtainable outside Athens supermarkets. Greeks eat no breakfast, so you need to bring something if you do not like the idea of cheese and olives first thing.

If you are ever near a monastery, you can ask for food and shelter there. You have to be modestly dressed, which means no shorts; and women are not allowed.

Getting on with people

Mountain people are extremely friendly and hospitable. It is, however, up to you, the stranger, to break the social ice by saying hello first. The simplest greetings are *kaleemèra,* good day, or *yàsoo,* good health to you *(yàsas* if there is more than one person). That immediately dispels what can appear to be hostility, but is in reality merely polite reserve. They are really dying to talk to you. You are like a new book or a new movie. They will talk about you for days after your departure. So make the most of your novelty!

Do not forget that they are very old-fashioned in their attitudes. Women, in particular, should be careful how they dress and act. Local women are not at all emancipated.

Weather/When to go

There is snow on the mountains from November to April. Quite extensive patches sometimes persist until mid-June and later on the higher and more northerly ones. The weather begins to settle in May and to break again at the beginning of October. July, August and September are the most settled months. They are also the hottest, but once you get into a big range like the Pindos, and high up, the heat is not bothersome. I have found my water frozen solid in the morning at 2000 metres near the Albanian border in September.

Certainly, the weather can be beautiful, but you should not be lulled into a false sense of security. Greek mountains behave like other mountains. Even in mid-summer, extremely violent storms can blow up with little warning. And nights are cool, especially in contrast to daytime temperatures.

What to take

In summer conditions, you need a combination of light and warm clothing. Shorts are essential and I would recommend a hat and shirts with collar and sleeves, if you are at all susceptible to sunburn. Take some protective cream for the vulnerable Anglo-Saxon nose and the backs of the knees. Warm clothing (including your sleeping bag) does not need to be heavy, just enough to protect you in bad weather and against the chill of tiredness and night. Take a windproof and waterproof cagoule. A good pair of lightweight Vibram-soled boots is sufficient in the way of footwear. Rigid-sole leather or plastic boots will be uncomfortably hot. Take a survival bag and basic first aid kit, including some mosquito repellent for use in the lowlands.

If you are packing a stove, make it a petrol-burner. Gas is not available outside the towns, whereas even in the remotest places there is usually at least a chainsaw that uses petrol.

Emergency services

There are not any. So do not have an accident. And if you do, pray for a speedy end on the mountainside. It will be less uncomfortable than the fate that awaits you in most clinics.

Getting to the mountains

Buses go everywhere in Greece. All major country towns have daily connections with Athens. Buses for the Peloponnese and parts of central Greece west of the Pindos mountains (Yànnina, for instance) leave from the terminus at 100 Kifíssou Street; to get there, take bus 051 from the corner of Vilarà and Menàndrou Streets near Omónia Square. Buses for Delphi, Àmfissa and parts east of the Pindos leave from 260 Liosion Street, near the Àyios Nikòlaos metro stop (or, take bus 029 from the National Gardens near Sìntagma Square). For information about bus times, ask at the tourist information desk in the National Bank of Greece on the corner of Sìntagma Square in Athens. Usually the only way to be absolutely certain is to go to the appropriate terminus.

From the country towns bone-jarring local buses set off for most villages, even the remotest . When there is not a bus, there is usually a village truck which takes passengers as well as goods. And, if you cannot get bus or truck, just step into the road and flag someone down. That is what the locals do. Vehicles are rare birds in out-of-the-way places, and you cannot afford not to make your intentions absolutely plain.

Using the book

This guide comprises accounts of one long (30-day) walk and various shorter ones, between one and five days in length. The long walk has been divided into three sections and could of course be further broken down.

The art of rendering Greek words in English letters is in a state of utter chaos. I have given Greek place names in the spelling you are most likely to encounter on road signs, with a guide to pronunciation in brackets (see Glossary). Where there is no bracketed pronunciation given, it means the normal spelling is a good enough guide by itself.

The estimates of walking times exclude halts and are records of my own times. There may have been occasions when I dawdled, but on the whole I got on with the job! I have long legs, know Greece very well and have usually been pretty fit. So it might be wise to allow a bit more time than I have. Wherever, for any reason, my record of my times and directions is uncertain, I have indicated it. Mt Athos is the main case, done in the days before I thought of a book.

L(eft) and R(ight) directions are given in relation to the walker's line of march. This applies also to the flanks of valleys and gullies. The only exception is actual stream or river banks, when L and R are indicated in relation to the direction of the current.

Abbreviations

EOT: Greek Tourist Organisation

HAC: Hellenic Alpine Club

NSSG: National Statistical Service of Greece

OTE: The Greek Telecommunications Organisation

Mt. Vardousia - the summit area above the refuge

Soufles peaks of Mt. Vardousia

PART TWO
Delphi to Albania

I have used Delphi as an eye-catcher. The route described really starts from Âmfissa, a small market town 25km west of Delphi, and runs from there right up the chain of the Pindos mountains to Mt.Grâmos on the Albanian frontier in the north-west corner of the province of Êpiros. It is more or less the same route as that followed by Lord Hunt's 1963 expedition. Total walking time is around 150 hours - approximately a month's walk.

The route follows the old mule trails and shepherds' paths that until recently were the only lines of communication between the mountain villages, and the rough bulldozer tracks that have replaced them, mostly since the 1950's. You will see only three tarmac roads in the whole journey. For most of the way you are travelling between 1000 and 2000 metres altitude. The highest point is 2637 metres, the summit of Mt.Smôlikas, west of the Epirot town of Kônitsa. The terrain is pretty rugged and some of the stages are unavoidably long and physically demanding. See the introduction for information about food and accommodation. Water is no problem. There are plenty of springs and streams, which are always safe to drink from, though it is as well to carry a good-sized water bottle and keep it topped up.

I have divided the route into three sections of a week to ten days' walking: Âmfissa to Karpenîsi, Karpenîsi to Mêtsovo and Mêtsovo to Mt.Grâmos. Karpenîsi and Mêtsovo both lie on the two major east-west roads across the mountains. Both have daily bus connections with Athens and are the easiest points of entry and exit. It is possible to get in or out of the mountains at other points, but once you are committed to a particular section of the route it is often no harder to go on than get out.

AMFISSA to ARTOTINA Scale: 1:200,000

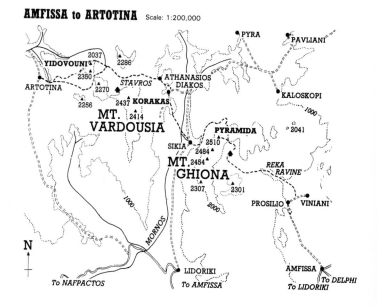

SECTION ONE: AMFISSA TO KARPENISI
Maps: NSSG 1:200,000   sheets Fokidos and Evrytanias
Total walking time: 43 hours.

There are daily buses to Àmfissa from Athens *(Odòs Liosìon terminus)*. It is a pleasant little town, situated at the edge of one of the largest olive plantations in Greece. It has a couple of hotels and restaurants, and a Frankish castle perched on a steep hill behind it. It used to be renowned for the manufacture of sheep-bells, and a few workshops are still in business - you cannot miss them for the clanging.

Àmfissa to Sikià across Mt.Ghiòna *(2510m)*
Walking time: 13½ hours.

This is a two-day hike, so stock up with provisions in Àmfissa *(àmfeesa)*. Don't overload, because it is a strenuous journey, involving an ascent of 2000 metres and an extremely steep descent of about 1400 metres - more, if you take in Pyramìda *(peeramèedha)*, the highest peak, on the way.

The route lies through the tiny village of Prosilio *(prosèelyo)*, where in summertime you might get something to eat, but it would be foolish to count on it. There is water, however.

Mt.Ghiòna *(gyòna)* is basically a long narrow rib of rock running north-south. Both flanks are steep, but the west face is a sheer wall of up to 1300 metres in height. The mountain is often climbed from the village of Kaloskopi, which lies to the north. The ascent described here is from the east via the deep and dramatic ravine of Rekà *(to faràngee tees rekàs)*.

There is a refuge hut *(katafèeyo)* beneath the Pyramìda peak in the area known as Làkka Karvoùni. However, it is such a palaver obtaining the key that it is better not to bother.

The Prosilio track leaves Àmfissa from the northern edge of town. From the square where the buses stop, go up the main street past the café Themis, round to the R of the church that blocks the way, and straight uphill towards the eastern (R) edge of the castle bluff.

In 15 minutes you come to a fork in front of the little church of Àyios Thanàssios. Bear L. In 5 minutes (20 mins) you have reached the last house. In front of you is a long valley, blocked directly ahead by a scrubby conical hill, but opening out to the west towards the rising bulk of Mt Ghiona.

The simplest thing is to follow the dirt road to Prosilio. There are, however, various short-cuts you can make by following the old path, and this is more agreeable. On the R past the last house a concrete bridge crosses a dry stream. There is a group of sheds on the further bank. A clear path leads round the back of the sheds, into an olive grove and steadily L, uphill, between low stone walls.

In 15 minutes (35 mins) you emerge on to open ground, where the path becomes a cart-track. 10 minutes (45 mins) later you rejoin the Prosilio road by some tumbledown sheepfolds at the foot of the scrubby conical hill.

Ahead is a gully marked with a scree of muck from the

Wood for the oven

construction of the road. Go straight up the gully. At the top of the scree you reach a wide platform where the road crosses (55 mins). Go up the L side of the dry stream at the back of the platform and work up L on to the road. Turn R on the road.

Just before the road crosses back R of the gully (now more a shallow valley), you come (1 hr 10 mins) to the remains of some terraced fields on the L. At the near edge of these fields a good path leads up L through the scrub, bringing you out on top of the ridge 15 minutes later (1hr 25 mins). You can see the road to your R.

10 minutes more (1hr 35 mins) bring you back to the road. A few paces on, just round the first bend, the path again strikes up L. Another few minutes and back to the road again. Now keep on it, up to the top of the ridge ahead of you (1hr 55 mins). Ghiòna is over to your L.

The road crosses the ridge in a cutting beneath some erect tooth-like rocks and, on the other side, descends the L flank of a steep, narrow gully with a stream in the bottom. Through a gap to the east you get a view of the western slopes of Mt Parnassos. Up ahead, on the next ridge, you get your first glimpse of fir trees.

In a few minutes (2 hrs 5 mins) you come to a bridge and, just beyond on the R, a spring in the shade of a group of plane trees. The road loops up to the ridge on your R and descends gently to Prosilio (3 hrs). To the east the ground drops away steeply into a big circular bowl, with the village of Viniani *(veenyanee)* in the bottom, surrounded by fields.

The name, Prosilio, means 'towards the sun'. The village lies at an altitude of about 1000 metres on the eastern slopes of Ghiòna looking out towards Parnassòs. The setting is magnificent. Huge planes shade the centre of the village. At its back a wooded ridge mounts steeply to the skyline. The lower slopes are dotted with sturdy stone houses built in the traditional mountain style, with wooden balconies over the main entrance, covered by a tiled porch supported on rough-hewn timbers.

The life of the place, however, has fled. Most of the houses lie half-buried in encroaching greenery. Ironically, it is probably the village's relative proximity to the outside world that has drained it of life more completely than some remoter places.

There is a fly blown *magazèe* beyond the village fountain, where the road begins to descend for Viniani.

It is more than 5½ hours to the Ghiòna refuge *(katafèeyo)*. Fill up with water, especially if you intend to camp in the Reka ravine. The nearest sure source of water is four hours away.

From Prosilio, go down the road, now a very rough track, towards Viniani. After about half an hour (30 mins) you pass a chapel on the L. Behind it, some way off, you can see the mouth of the ravine.

Quarter of an hour beyond the chapel (45 mins), a variety of goat paths go off L through the scrub. Take one and aim straight across country to the mouth of Reka (55 mins).

The ravine begins abruptly at the edge of a riverside meadow. The gravelly, dry bed of the river fills the ravine from side to side. There is no room for a path. You walk up the floor of the ravine. The walls of the ravine become rapidly higher and closer, until it forms a narrow trench some 300 or 400 metres deep cutting right into the heart of the mountain. Trees and shrubs lean out precariously from its nearly sheer walls. But it is no good trying to divert yourself with Gothic imaginings inspired by the scenery. The unevenness of the river bed obliges you to keep your eyes glued to the dizzying passage of

Mt. Ghiona - approaching the refuge

white stones under your feet, like watching a perverse kind of conveyor belt that leaves you to do all the work. And it is hard work. The loose gravel shifts under your feet like dry sand. The ravine twists and turns, climbing all the time. You realise how quickly you have been gaining height by the presence of firs right down at the edge of the river-bed.

About 1¾ hours up the ravine (2 hrs 40 mins), after a series of bends, you come to a place where it opens out a bit. There is a terrace of flat firm ground on the R for the first time, with fir trees growing along it. On the L a steep slope of tumbled boulders leads up to the base of a rock wall cut by a dark narrow cleft, perhaps 100 metres high and only 4 wide.

It is a good place to camp. There are some comfortable patches of fine sandy gravel to bed down on, and plenty of wood to make a fire. There are no rules about lighting fires - there are no rules about anything! Just be careful, and be sure to put your fire out properly before going on.

20 minutes beyond this spot (3 hrs), at the foot of an enormous rock wall, you come to a wide bowl-shaped opening in the ravine, where the main river swings L into a narrow wooded defile and a steep tributary gully runs down off the heights to the R. There is a

clear path here, running along the top of a low retaining wall. Follow the path into the defile, keeping to the R bank.

At the further end (3 hrs 15 mins) there is a substantial stone wall on the opposite bank. The path crosses to the L and climbs steeply up an open stony slope. At the top it levels out and peters out. You find yourself once more trudging along in the gravelly river-bed under the firs.

50 minutes later (4 hrs 5 mins) you come to a great red cliff on the L, dripping with water and verdant with hanging plants. Clamber up the scree to its base and you will find an abundant spring.

From here on the path shows clearly. In summertime there should be dollops of mule shit to reassure you!

About 20 minutes beyond the red cliff (4 hrs 25 mins) you emerge from the shade of the firs into a wide sunny place where the sides of the ravine at last recede. Here you get your first glimpse of the summit ridge *(koreefogrammèe)* of Ghióna, a long grey wall of rock towering ahead of you, jagged with numerous peaks over 2300 metres. To the L (south) of this line of peaks and standing somewhat apart is the tower-like peak of Profitis Ilias *(profèetees eelèeyas.)*

The river describes a substantial curve to the L. On the R of this bend is a hard flat terrace of ground where a stream debouches from a narrow wooded gully.

Do not continue up the main river; you will find the way completely blocked after about half an hour. The path for the *katafèeyo* climbs up the spine of the wooded spur dividing the course of the main river from the new tributary gully, pretty well bisecting the angle of junction.

Be careful. The path does not show up on the hard ground on your R. Cast about patiently until you pick it up at the edge of the firs, where the ground begins to rise. There is a very small cairn of stones to mark the beginning of the path, but it is easily missed. The path is steep and reasonably well marked by the passage of hooves. Shepherds go up and down this way is summer, though not as often as formerly, because jeep tracks opened up by a mining company give easier access from the north side of the mountain.

The path strays a bit L and R of the spine of the spur. If you are uncertain, stick to the spine as a guide. As you approach the tree-line, you catch a glimpse of the pink-tiled roof of the *katafèeyo* away through the trees at the head of the deepening gully on your R.

20 minutes' climb (4 hrs 45 mins) brings you out above the tree-line in a patch of meadow full of brilliant red flowers of dianthus biflorus, magenta-coloured geranium subcaulescens and white cerastium candidissimus.

From here a clear path bears R, keeping close to the tree-line all along the base of the summit ridge. The *katafèeyo* is in view all the way. You reach it in about 55 minutes (5 hrs 40 mins).

There is an enormous boulder at one end of the *katafèeyo,* taller than the building itself, and between the two is a rickety shepherd's hut *(kalèeva).* There is another sheepfold *(stròonga)* a couple of hundred metres away on the other side of the refuge too. Either of them might give you something to eat, and would certainly help out with any difficulties.

Above the *katafèeyo,* the summit ridge rises to its highest point in the Pyramida peak (2510m), so called because it is roughly pyramidal. To the north (R) of it, the ridge drops into the col of Skasmàda *(to dheeyàselo tees skasmàdhas)* and curves round to terminate in the lower peak of Kakovòuni *(kakovòonee.)* These two peaks and the col together enfold a corrie *(làka,)* which lies directly behind the refuge.

The way to Sikiá *(Seekyà)* (4½ hrs) lies over the col of Skasmàdha. When asking for directions, ask for Lazòrema, the Làzos stream, for that is your vital descent route. There is not any other. Stand with you back to the refuge, facing Kakovòuni. On the grassy slope just below the crags at the R edge of Kakovòuni two large white boulders *(kotrònes)* lying a little apart stand out quite distinctly. Aim for these. A narrow path runs behind them and up L across the screes to the R corner of the col.

Go down into the hollow behind the refuge and follow up the stream-bed, where you will see red marks painted on the rocks by the HAC (Hellenic Alpine Club) to indicate the route to the refuge from the north. From the stream you have to make your own way up to the foot of Kakovòuni; there is no obvious path.

It takes about 35 minutes to reach the boulders. There you pick up the path which takes you up across the screes below the rocks of Kakavòuni. Towards the top of the col the path winds through tall jagged outcrops.

On the col, which you reach about 40 minutes after the boulders (1 hr 15 mins), a chill wind invariably greets you. The altitude is about 2100 metres. A superb view opens out to the north and west. To the north is Mt Oíti with the village of Pyrà visible on its lower slopes. Far off in the north-west, over the intervening ridges and peaks, you can see the distinctive conical shape of Mt Velôuchi, which overlooks the town of Karpenísi. Beyond lie the heights of Ágrafa, the merest fudge of blue at this distance. To the west, and close at hand, you can see the northern half of the Vardóusia massif separated from you by the deep valley of the Mórnos river. The southern half is hidden by the beetling north crags of Pyramìda, which rises steeply from the col at your L elbow. Sikià too lies hidden round that corner and some 1400 metres lower down.

At your feet the close alpine turf slopes gently down to a grassy meadow in a hollow at the foot of Pyramìda. Just below the col a gully develops and you follow a path down the R side of it. At the edge of the meadow there is a large overhanging rock, in whose shade a thick wedge of snow lies until late in the year. Round its melting edges, even in July, there are glossy blue Alpine Squills and crocus veluchensis still in flower. Just beyond is the Gòuvalis family's *stròonga,* a better organised and more prosperous-looking outfit than the one by the refuge.

It is an idyllic spot, especially in the evening when the late sun gilds the backs of the sheep and glistens on the grass and the stream of snow-melt that threads across the meadow from the foot of Pyramìda, and the harmonious chiming of the sheep-bells lends an air of quiet and private domesticity to what is essentially a wild and inhospitable place. It would make a fine base camp for exploring the whole summit area of Ghiôna, which is, incidentally, unusually rich in fossils.

From the Gòuvalis *stròonga* you cross the meadow, go over the low grassy ridge bounding its western edge and down a slope, where there is yet another *stròonga.* (As I went by the old shepherd called me over to pass the time of day. Leaning on his crook, his creased and weathered face thrust myopically close to mine, he asked, *'Tee yêenesthe?* How are you? *Apô pou èrhesthe?* Where have you come from? *Pou tha pàte?* Where are you going?' Satisfied on these points, he went on to ask about the war in the 'Faklans ... what do you call them? Anyway, what do you want those islands for? They're far away, desert ...' I answered in a non-committal way. 'And why do you let yourselves be governed by a woman? Aren't there any men in the country? It's not right. They're unstable!' He sighed. *'Tee na kânoume?* What can we do about it? We're all in the hands of God. He made us and when we don't do what He ordains He punishes us

Mt. Ghiona from the west

with wars and suffering. *Ètsee dhen èene? Isn't that so?'*)

At the bottom of this slope a gully goes down to the L between two rocky bluffs. A stream rises in the gully, cutting a narrow twisty channel in the turf; this is the beginning of Lazórema. In July there is no more than a trickle of water, which quickly vanishes.

Go L down the gully. In a few minutes you find yourself looking over the edge of a very steep, rocky descent. This is the way the stream goes, and there is no other.

Pyramìda and the crags of the west face of Ghióna now rise sheer above you on the L. On your R a long wooded ridge runs out parallel to these, hiding the Mórnos valley from view. You are facing south, looking back down the flank of Ghióna. Way below your feet and slightly R as you look down Lazórema, you can see patches of lighter green showing through the dark of the fir trees. This is the locality known as Làzos, where once the villagers of Sikià used to cultivate fields. Now it is fallow, a beautiful bowl-shaped meadow. Sikià itself lies out of sight below the end of the ridge on your R. Your route lies through the Làzos meadow and out through the gap cut by the Lazórema stream between this ridge and the cliffs of Ghióna.

The descent of Lazórema is tiring and uncomfortable. There is a great deal of loose rock. With the stream running it could be very awkward. It takes about one hour (3 hrs) to reach the bottom of the steep section (1 hr 25 mins from the Gòuvalis *stròonga*).

At the bottom of this section, the stream makes a right-angle junction with another steep gully coming down from the L off the base of the cliffs above. The best route is straight across the junction on to the opposite bank of the combined streams, where there is a small grassy clearing in the edge of the wood. There is no obvious path. Turn into the trees and downhill, keeping no more than 50 metres from L bank of Lazórema. There are a number of unconvincing paths under the trees. Just continue down close to the gully and in about 15 minutes (3 hrs 15 mins) you come to a junction with another gully coming in from the R with a permanent stream in it. A path materialises under your feet and turns downhill to the L through firs and patches of grass, following the line of the stream.

In 10 minutes (3 hrs 25 mins) you come to the Lázos meadows, ringed by dark firs and overshadowed by the cliffs of Ghiòna now towering 1000 metres or more above you. This too would make an ideal camp site. There is a *stròonga* on the bank of the stream where you could get milk and cheese.

The path through the meadow runs along above the L bank of the stream gully, which rapidly develops into a sizeable ravine. At the further edge of the meadow you come out on a steep slope of rock and scree, with scattered firs, high above the mouth of the ravine. The village of Sikià is visible below you to the R.

Descend the scree and at the bottom strike out in a more or less straight line for the village. The path runs close to a water conduit *(eedhragoyèeo)*. You reach the village in just over one hour from the Lazos *stròonga* (4 hrs 35 mins).

Sikià *(seekyà)* is a small village lying astride the dirt road that runs north from the market town of Lidoriki *(leedhorèekee)* up the Mòrnos river valley to the foot of Mt Oiti, where it branches in various directions east and west. The village is situated at an altitude of just under 900 metres, at the lower limit of the fir tree zone. It is a verdant little place, full of leafy planes, in a dramatic setting, with the cliffs of Ghiòna at its back and the jagged heights of Vardòusia in front.

It can be reached directly from Lidoriki, which has a daily bus service to Athens. Transport on from Lidoriki is irregular. It takes about 3½ hours to do the journey on foot. It is not a very interesting walk, although to begin with at least you can enjoy the view of the lake that has recently been created by damming the Mórnos river at the southern tip of Mt Vardóusia. The lake supplies water to Athens via a pipeline, which you may have noticed crossing the hillside below Delphi as you came through. One or two half-submerged buildings are visible above the water; they are all that remains of the village of Kallió. The project is not popular with local people, because it has cut them off from their traditional trade with the mountain hinterland west of Vardóusia, whose villages now communicate more easily with Náfpactos.

Sikià has two *magazyà* in the centre of the village by the church. Both can fix you a meal. The *magazèe* on the road also has accommodation.

Sikià to Athanàssios Diakos

Walking time: 4½ hours

Local people continue to say Ano (Upper) Moussounitsa *(àno moosoonèetsa)* although the village has been officially renamed Athanàssios Diàkos after a nationalist hero of the war of independence, and appears on the map under this latter name.

It lies high on the west flank of the Mórnos valley a little to the north of Sikià. It is the kicking-off point for ascents of Vardóusia.

The easiest way to get to it is by road - about 4 hours' walk. 1½ hours north of Sikià you come to a crossroads with a signpost pointing L to Athanàssios Diàkos (8km). There is a spring a few paces down this turning. After a 20 minute descent you come to a bridge over the Mórnos (nice pool with trout below the bridge: good for a lunch stop). An hour's steep climb brings you to Kàto (Lower) Moussounitsa, where you bear R, and a further hour takes you over a thickly wooded ridge and down to Àno Moussounitsa.

There is also a path, which takes a bit longer, is trickier to find, but is more fun!

Start by standing on the edge of the square *(platèeya)* in Sikià and looking out west across the valley.

At your R shoulder the Lazórema stream comes down from Ghióna and flows down the broad gully in front of you to join the Mórnos river in the valley bottom. On the further bank of the Mórnos, just upstream (R) from this junction, you can clearly see

31

two light green patches of plane trees marking two stream gullies. Follow the Lazórema down to the river, cross over and aim for the R-hand green gully. Above it and slightly to the R you can see some rocky outcrops on a scrub-covered spur which climbs up the valley side almost as far as the scar of the Koniàkos-Kàto Moussounìtsa road, which is clearly visible crossing the flank of Vardousia at the lower limit of the fir trees. From the river you climb up to the road keeping just to the L of this spur. Near the top you pass through some disused fields *(horàfya)*.

The path leads out of the L corner of the *platèeya,* down between tiny walled plots of maize, vines and beans. Over to the R, the far bank of Lazórema is pitted with caves, which the locals have used as shelters for livestock or store-houses. Ahead of you rise the peaks of Vardôusia.

At first the path winds down L of Lazórema, then bears R to cross it and continue down the R bank. On the further bank you pass through small patches of hay, where hundreds of butterflies bask: Swallowtails, Camberwell Beauties, Blues and Graylings. Half an hour after starting (30 mins) you come to a bucolic spot worthy of Theocritus.

Past an ancient thorn tree entwined with wild vine you descend a dozen paces to the foot of a grassy bank, where from beneath a rock a full-fledged stream slides silently into the sunlight. On the edge of the bank a clump of crimson poppies is sharply silhouetted against the hazy blue shadow of the mountain behind. Walnut trees spread their heavy shade all round and the bushes are festooned with coils of Old Man's Beard. It is a place for a bathe and a bite. Fill up with water.

3 minutes further on you cross another stream under plane trees, and then the path comes out above the Mórnos. It is significantly hotter in the bottom of the valley. The vegetation, from being rather lush, changes to prickly oak scrub *(poornàreeya)* and underfoot the ground becomes shaly. You can plainly see the gully you are aiming for on the other side of the river.

In 10 minutes (45 mins) the path turns down along the side of a stream to the river-bed. Cross the river in the direction of the R-hand of the two gullies you saw from Sikíà. The main water channel runs close to the west bank and has to be waded. It is roughly knee-deep and 25 metres across in early July (1 hr).

When you reach the R-hand gully you will find there is no path.

32

Climb out on to the apparent R bank of the gully and prepare, if it is a hot day, for the most unpleasant hour of your holiday!

There are numerous sheep runs on the gritty ground, but none leads anywhere. It is impossible to get a general sense of the way ahead, for the irregular patches of open ground are hemmed in by thick brakes of scrub and evergreen oak, which pour prickly leaves down your neck every time you nudge a branch with your rucksack. The only thing is to try not to stray too far to the L and keep as close as possible to the crown of the spur.

I got too far over to the L and had to clamber back to the R up a horribly steep earth bank, which sapped my last reserves of will power. Just as I was about to do violence to my companion we came to a tiny pool of clear water (1 hr 40 mins) at the foot of a plane tree. It was surrounded by moss and grass and fed by such gentle subterranean pressure that not a ripple showed on its surface. We lay in the shade reviving ourselves by pouring spring water over our heads, and enjoying the superb view all down the Mórnos valley to the blue waters of the lake at Lidoriki.

Only a few minutes higher up we found the fields we had been told about, just on the line of the spur. I suspect there must be a good path directly from the top of these fields to the road; it would be worth casting about to find it.

We went out of the top L corner of the fields into a dry gully and turned R up the apparent L bank along what appeared to be a path. It soon petered out in the stones of the stream-bed, so we crossed over and scrambled up the shaly bank opposite. A little way up, we hit an overgrown but once well-used trail, which led us to a fence enclosing a plantation of young walnut trees. We followed the fence uphill until it brought us out in a patch of meadow right beside the road (2 hrs 5 mins).

Turn R on the road, uphill, into the trees. It is easy going. You pass a turning back L to Koniàkos; keep on R. After 35 minutes steady going (2 hrs 40 mins), rounding a bend in the road, you get your first glimpse of Kàto Moussounitsa lying some way below at the head of a gully. On the far side of it is the road up from Sikià.

Keep your eyes open for the path. It leaves the road on the R just past this bend and cuts down through the trees. A few paces on you hit the road again. Cross over and pick up the path once more. It takes you down over shaly gullies in open woodland to the village in 30 minutes (3 hrs 10 mins), and is much quicker than flogging round by the road.

In the village the path takes you past the *magazèe*. Stop: it is a pretty one, with a vine-shaded terrace looking out over the valley. There is an attractive freshness and lushness about Kâto Moussounitsa, with its garden plots overflowing with greenery. Being small and off the beaten track it has remained untouched by modernity.

You can go on to Ano Moussounitsa by road, but there is an attractive path, which it would be a shame to miss.

Turn up the path along the side of the *magazèe* and go on out of the top of the village, until you reach the Koniâkos road again in 15 minutes (3 hrs 25 mins). Turn R on the road and almost at once you come to a culvert over a stream. Literally five paces before the culvert, a path goes up into the woods on the L.

In 20 minutes (3 hrs 45 mins) you come to a stream in a glade of planes - a lovely spot in the evening sun. 10 minutes later you reach the top of the ridge, still in the forest. There is a fine view behind you back to Ghiðna.

Another quarter of an hour (4 hrs 10 mins) and you come out on the road. Turn L. The houses of Áno Moussounítsa are now visible on your R. The advance buttresses and screes of Kôrakas (2485 metres), Vardôusia's highest peak, rise brooding above you, blocking out the western sky and casting long evening shadows over the village. A deep boulder-strewn gully has been gouged out of the R flank of the peak, and down it pours a cold, green torrent, which you cross at the entrance to the village (4 hrs 20 mins). Another good place for a bathe.

Āno Moussounítsa/Athanâssios Diâkos is a luxuriant oasis of broad-leaved green amid the dark firs which surround it. It is full of planes and sweet chestnuts, whose pale gold candles are a splendid sight in flower in early July.

The village itself does not measure up to the beauty of its surroundings. You would not call it thriving, but it does seem to attract enough people in summer, emigré native sons and shepherds, to keep it from total decline.

The *platèeya,* whose best feature by far is two grand old planes with fountains at their base, has been largely rebuilt. There is one old-fashioned *magazèe* left, patronised chiefly by the old-timers. A severe-looking stone church with frosted glass doors stands to one

34

side. There is an unimpressive monument to Athanássios Diákos, the village's illustrious son, who was impaled (by the Turks) on a spit and roasted alive for refusing to renounce his Christian faith. In the R corner is the village hostelry: a glass and brass taverna with blown-up photos of New England in the fall, and a pink concrete annex with beds. The food is simple, good and plentiful, the accomodation clean, and the people nice.

Athanássios Diákos to Artotina across Mt Vardóusia (2405m)

Walking time: 8 hours

The Vardóusia *(vardhóosya)* massif - one of the most interesting mountain areas in Greece for both walker and climber - forms a long thin triangle with its apex to the south resting on the artificial lake created by the Mórnos River dam at Lidoriki. Its more than 40 peaks over 2000 metres - the Greek equivalent of the Munro - are arranged in three groups round a beautiful central area of sloping pastures. Unusually rocky and precipitous they are a favourite stamping ground for Greek climbers. Some, which is rare in Greece, are accessible only to the rock-climber.

There are two refuge huts at the base of the eastern group of peaks, about 3 hours' walk from Áno Moussounitsa. They make a good base for exploring the range, although in summer of course you can easily camp out. There is plenty of water. Between June and October there are several sheepfolds in the area, which would certainly help out with provisions. Also, most of the shepherds have pick-up trucks and will readily give you a lift down to the village.

Kórakas (2495m), the highest peak in the massif, is 3 hours' climb from the huts. The route goes up the scree directly above the upper hut, through a couloir known as Pórtes (gates) and out on to the small plateau of Méga Kámbos. From there you can see the summit at the top of the skyline ridge on your R.

To get to Artotina *(artotéena),* the first objective is the col of Stavrós, the very obvious gap in the ridge directly above the village.

From the *platéeya* return to the track by which you arrived. To the R it continues up to Stavrós: that is the route the shepherds now use with their trucks. As usual, however, the old path is quicker and more interesting for the walker.

So, turn L along the track for a few paces, until you come to a short, muddy, tree-lined gully on the R. At the back of the gully a path goes up L through bushes of yellow broom, round behind a small building in whose bowels the sounds of rushing water are clearly audible, and on to the main trail. Turn L.

Follow the clear stony path uphill through the fir trees until you hit the track (40 mins). Turn L and follow the track to the first sharp R-hand bend (50 mins). On the crown of the bend the path turns off L into the trees, keeps along the level for a few paces, then turns sharply uphill to the R. For about 25 minutes you labour up a steep awkward bank with a deep gully on your L. At the top of the bank you come out in a grassy level clearing by a small stone shrine *(eekòneesma)* dedicated to Profitis Ilias (the prophet Elijah) (1 hr 15 mins). There is a spring in the clearing. Should it be dry, there is more water higher up.

If you are aiming for the huts, continue up the track for about 200 metres. Where the track bends R, the path continues straight uphill, marked by splashes of green paint. It ascends a series of grassy hillocks, keeping always to the L above the track, then bears L round the base of the rocky heights that mark the northern end of the Korakas group of peaks. The lower of the two huts comes into view quite soon. You approach it along the top of a low ridge overlooking the Pittimàliko meadows stretching away to your R. The upper hut is about 2 hours from the Profitis Ilias shrine.

For Artotina, cut down to the track when you reach the col, about 1 hour above the shrine (2 hrs 15 mins). From Stavròs, the ground slopes away westwards and northwards, reaching its lowest point in the pasture known as Skasmèni *(skasmènee),* where the shepherds' track ends. There the Karyòtiko stream, which rises in these pastures and later becomes the river Evinòs or Fidaris *(Snake River),* plunges into a ravine which leads out of the north-west corner of the massif. Facing you across the gully of the infant stream is a wall of high peaks, in the middle of which is a very distinctive gap, the col known as *èe dheeyàsela too vardhoòsee.* This is the way out to Artotina. To your L are the rocky bulwarks that hide Kòrakas from view, to your R the long ridge of Sinàni that encloses the northern edge of the meadows.

From Stavròs, follow the track to its end at Skasmèni (3 hrs). There cut down by the sheepfold on the L to the stream. On the far bank, a grassy slope dotted with boulders and rocky outcrops reaches up to the foot of a long wall of rock. The col is directly above you to the L or south of it is the Alogòrahi peak *(alogòrahee* - horse ridge); to the north is, first, Pyramida *(peeramèedha),* then the very-

Spinning

red looking Yidovoúni *(yeedhovòonee)* or Goat Mountain, with a high step-like col between them.

(An alternative route to Artotina turns the northern flank of Yidovoúni. Keep as close to the foot of the crags as possible, just on or above the timberline. Once round the end, follow the foot of the crags back in a south-westerly direction until you meet a path bearing diagonally R across to a long wooded spur running out west. A small white shrine is visible towards the end of the spur. From the crown of the spur, the path runs west along its south-facing flank, bears R in open ground below the limit of the fir trees and drops down through abandoned terraces into the valley bottom below Artotina. The village is in view from the time you begin to descend the flank of the valley. It is about 4 hours from Skasméni.)

From the stream below Skasméni head straight uphill to the main col (4 hrs 30 mins). There is no particular path, though a small stream provides a good line. It is a particularly beautiful climb on a June or July morning with the first sun on your back. The turf is springy and soft and full of flowers; pinks, geraniums, edraianthus, marsh orchids. In the meadows below, flocks of sheep move down to their pens for the morning milking, bells chiming harmoniously. The western flanks of Kôrakas are still blue with shadow.

From the col, you look west down into an enormous cirque with a flattish grassy floor with a shepherd's hut in the middle. The most impressive of the peaks enclosing the cirque are the four Soúfles *(soofles)* off to your L; they have been honed by the weather into sharp-pointed teeth. The only exit from the ring of peaks is down the narrow ravine of the Vardousiótiko stream *(vardhoosyóteeko),* which flows due west to Artotina.

From the col, bear down L across steep screes, aiming for the shepherd's hut. At the bottom you cross two streams and climb a low bank on to the meadows round the sheepfold (5 hrs 30 mins). From the *stróonga* a path leads across the meadows into the corner formed by the Vardousiótiko ravine and the Kostarîtsa peak which closes the western side of the cirque. There, the way ahead is blocked by a projecting buttress of rock and the path zigzags down the side of the ravine to a lower level before continuing westwards close to the timberline. Gradually you drop down into the trees until (6 hrs 50 mins) you come to the edge of a steep bluff overlooking patches of green field. A water channel appears beside the path at this point and splashes downhill beside it.

At the foot of the bluff the path levels out above the L bank of the Vardousiótiko stream. The fir trees give way to oak, hazel and plane. Abandoned terraces rank with grass, brambles and Old Man's Beard lie beside the path. In 50 minutes (7 hrs 40 mins) you come to the confluence of the Vardousiótiko and Artotína streams (the latter apparently nameless). Shortly before the confluence there are several good bathing places close to the path.

Cross the Artotína stream, turn L up the track on the far side for a few paces, then R up a steep bank on to a path that leads uphill through unkempt fields to the first houses of the village (8 hrs).

By mountain standards Artotína is a substantial village, its houses scattered widely over a large area of hill-side round the 1200-metre contour. There has been some rebuilding in the centre of the village, but many of the pretty old stone houses survive, with stone-tiled roofs and wooden galleries at first floor level.

The *platéeya,* as usual, is the hub of village life with two or three tree-shaded *magazyà* along one side and a church in the middle. In the hollow behind the square is an old blue-shuttered house which serves as a guest house - primitive but tolerable. In the lane leading uphill from the square is a taverna where a meal of sorts can be had.

The area is known as Little Switzerland *(mikrèe elvetéeya).* Looking back at the Vardòusia mountains to the cirque below the Sòufles peaks you understand why. It is as dramatic a mountain view as you can find in Greece.

During the 1946-49 civil war there were bloody clashes in the surrounding mountains between Communist guerrillas and so-called nationalist forces. Opposite the church is a memorial to gendarmes killed in one of these engagements. There is no memorial, of course, to the guerrillas who were also Greeks; they are simply referred to as 'bandits'.

Artotina to Gramèni Oxià

Walking time: 3 hours

Leave Artotina by the dirt road, heading north. Just outside the village, by the cemetery (R), the road enters the trees. 15 minutes from the village square a clear path leaves the road on the R. You pass a chapel - Àyios Spirìdona - on the R (20 mins) and a sign pointing L to the 'sacred library' - though you wonder what sort of library might be located in the middle of these remote woods. There is a spring on the L at 25 mins and at 40 mins you rejoin the road.

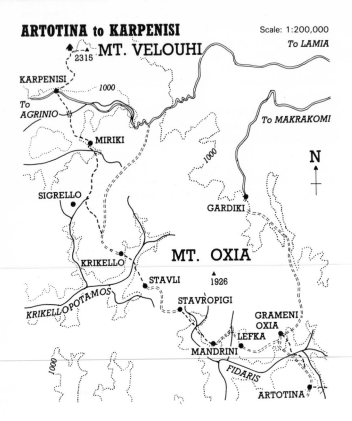

ARTOTINA to KARPENISI

Scale: 1:200,000

To LAMIA

MT. VELOUHI

2315

KARPENISI

1000

To AGRINIO

To MAKRAKOMI

MIRIKI

1000

N

SIGRELLO

GARDIKI

MT. OXIA

KRIKELLO

STAVLI

1926

KRIKELLOPOTAMOS

STAVROPIGI

GRAMENI OXIA

LEFKA

1000

MANDRINI

FIDARIS

ARTOTINA

Turn R. The woods are full of sweet chestnuts here. At 55 mins you pass a walled fountain in the crook of a sharp R bend. 10 minutes later (1 hr 5 mins), still on the road, you come to the lovely but now deserted monastery of Åyios Yànnis. The church, unfortunately, is usually locked. At the top of some steps, beneath a plane tree, is a house where the martyred Athanàssios Diàkos lived as a young novice. Below the monastery, on the L round the next bend in the road, is a small pink-roofed chapel (1 hr 15 mins). A path passes in front of it, crosses the road a few moments later and goes straight on down through fir, chestnut and oak towards the bottom of the valley

40

of the river Fídaris *(fĕedharees).*

The path first turns back towards the R, then swings L. At a fork, a branch path to the R leads down to overgrown 'fields' on the true L bank of the Fídaris stream (1 hr 30 mins). Opposite is a gully which comes down from Gramĕni Oxià *(gramĕnee oxyà).* (I suspect it is better to go straight on at the fork rather than take the branch path. In any case, either path is preferable to the road which makes a long detour downstream before coming back to the ford.)

Turn downstream along the L bank until you reach the telphone line. Cross the river under the telephone line and continue downstream on the R bank until you hit the road by the piles of a bridge which has remained unfinished for years (1 hr 50 mins). It was apparently promised by a local MP in an effort to win votes, then simply abandoned. It is a cause of mirth and bitterness locally, for in winter the villages north of the Fídaris are cut off.

80 paces up the road a path leads R up a steep bank. Don't miss it; it is a good path and miles shorter than the road. You meet the road again in the middle of a hairpin bend enclosing a modern chapel. Immediately past the crown of the bend the path continues on the R. A stone chapel stands beside the path (L) at 2 hrs 6 mins. On the R are fields and the telephone line. 15 minutes later (2 hrs 21 mins) you reach the houses of the lower quarter of Gramĕni Oxià *(kàto mahalàs):* as primitive a place as you are likely to see - a few ancient dilapidated houses without water or electricity, half-buried in greenery and inhabited by a handful of old-timers whose lives belong more to the 15th than 20th century.

Thence, 40 minutes' steep climb brings you to the road at the entrance to Gramĕni Oxià. Turn R into Gramĕni Oxià (3 hrs), another pretty but run-down mountain village lying at about 1100 metres on the northern slopes of the Fídaris valley, looking southeast towards Vardòusia.

There are two *magazyà,* one in the square, one on the 'main' street. The latter has rooms for the night, as does the house next door.

There is a bus service in summer. An ancient Mercedes leaves the village at 5 a.m. and grinds over a mountain track to Makrakòmi in the Spèrchios river valley on the Lamìa·Karpenìsi road. There is room for a dozen passengers, plus half a dozen sheep or a bundle of hay.

The village's name means the 'inscribed beech tree'. There are extensive beech woods on the heights above the village and legend has it that one of them was marked and used as a meeting place by the roaming outlaw bands that lived in the hills and fought the Turks in the days before the independence of the Greek state. It is a not uncommon name throughout the Greek mountains.

A marvellous alternative route to Karpenísi would be due north along the ridge above Gramèni Oxià to join the Lamía-Karpenísi road above the village of Timfristos. It was the route in the old days and looks - from a distance - to be fairly level pegging along grassy rounded tops at about 1700 metres. About a day's march.

Gramèni Oxià to Lèfka

Walking time: 1¼ hours

Leave Gramèni Oxià by the road, heading west. At the junction beyond the last houses turn uphill to the R - signposted Lèfka 7km. The track passes a plantation of young firs on the R, then follows the 1200-metre contour along the north side of the Fidaris valley. At 50 mins you pass a chapel on the L, with woods of oak above and below the road. At 1 hr 5 mins, rounding a R-hand bend, you come in sight of the village of Kydonià on the far side of the valley. Further off to the south west is Dendrohòri. Lèfka is in sight below you on the R. To your L is a chapel on a spur. A path leads down R of the road cutting off the last corners. You come to some primitive houses among fir trees, then shortly after hit the road by a curious white marble relief depicting sheep and a man on horseback dressed like a cowboy. It is dedicated to one Vlahoyànnis, who paid for the restoration of the church.

At 1 hr 15 mins you reach the *platèeya,* a concrete apron built out round the church and facing west across a ravine.

The name Lèfka means poplar tree, and there are indeed a number of poplars on the slopes below the village. The old, however, still call it by its Slav name, *meekrèe palòokoova.*

It is very derelict and quite deserted in the winter months except for a creature described to me as being 'somewhat lopsided', i.e. crazy. One or two families have begun to repair their houses for use as summer homes - refuges from the smog of Athens and Piraeus.

There is a *magazèe* beside the church. The *magazèes,* having offered me *patsàs* for breakfast (a soup made of the unmentionable bits of a cow, just about palatable when dowsed with vinegar and considered a great delicacy), inquired what I was doing. When I answered, 'Walking to Karpenisi', a tipsy builder said, 'What sort of a bloody awful country is it that can't even offer a fellow a road to travel on?' I said, 'It's nice to walk.' A man who had lost a leg in the civil war said, 'If you have legs.' The *magazées,* explaining my eccentricity to the others, said, 'He doesn't want cars and mod. cons. That's why he comes here.' At this point a rather pretty and sexy young girl in a tee-shirt rode up on a Honda. No one seemed surprised. A scene worthy of Bunuel!

Lefka to Mandrini

Walking time: 1¼ hours

Along the track again, although it is hardly more than a sandy path now, innocent of traffic except for the postman's bike. At Mandrinì *(mandhreenèe)* it peters out altogether.

From the *platèeya* in Lèfka cut straight down over the open ground at your feet, ignoring the track, until you meet it again at the lowest point visible from the *platèeya* on a sharp R-hand bend. Just round the bend cut down L again. When you next hit the track, turn R and follow it down to the ford over the stream in the bottom of the ravine (25 mins). Cross the stream and climb steadily back uphill, regaining the 200 metres (or so) you have lost in the descent from Lèfka. Abandoned fields rank with vegetation border the track. Walnut trees abound.

At 1 hr the chapel of Àyios Athanàssios stands in a walled graveyard L of the track on the edge of a spur jutting out above the confluence of three streams. The village of Livadàki is visible on the mountainside to the west, surrounded by an unbroken expanse of dark forest. At 1 hr 15 mins you enter Mandrinì, formerly known as *megàlee palòokoova,* a tiny village of old stone houses grouped round the church, also inhabited only in summer. Asked where I had come from, I replied nonchalantly that I had walked up from Lidorìki and was promptly put in my place by an old lady who said that in her youth she used to go down to Lidorìki in nine hours to sell maize at 2 *grossia* (a Turkish coin, but used by the old-timers to mean drachmas) the *okà* (an old measure of weight equivalent to 1, 2kg). So much for those of us who walk for sport!

Mandrinì to Stavropigi

Walking time: 1¾ hours

Leave Mandrinì by the continuation of the track. After a very short distance, just 2 or 3 minutes from the church, 20 paces before the track bends R and out of sight of the village, a path goes down to the L. Well-trodden and pretty, it drops down the east side of a ravine formed by a tributary of the Fidaris, through oak, scrub oak, juniper and fir. In 30 minutes, you come to a bank of overgrown terraces just above the river bank.

Be careful here. I would certainly have got lost without a good share of luck. They had told me in Mandrinì to look out for Petros the miller, who was working in his fields by the river. Just below the lowest terrace is a watermill hidden in the trees. Luckily the miller was there with another old man, sharpening an ancient saw, while the mill racketted away grinding some maize flour.

The mill is a fascinating relic, the last of its kind in the area. It was made by Petros' father, probably around 1910. A channel brings stream water to the head of a wooden chute above the mill, which is about the size of a small single-roomed cottage. The chute provides the necessary force to turn the water-wheel, which is connected by primitive wooden gears and a massive axle made from a squared-off tree trunk to the millstones inside the cottage. The whole structure was fashioned by eye with an adze. The parts are held together by wooden wedges. 'Crude work,' was Petros' comment, 'but you have to know how'. I'll say!

Below the mill is a second chute connected to a wooden basin set in the ground, used in the treatment of *flokàtes,* the loose-woven shaggy woollen rugs that are now a popular Greek export. A good pounding and soaking in water tightens and thickens the weave, giving the rugs a felt-like backing.

Luckily for me, the second old man was going to Stavropigi *(stavropeeyèe)* with his mule and load of flour. You are not likely to be so lucky! So take your time over the next 15 to 20 minutes.

From the mill, go down on to the stony banks of the river and head upstream for a few paces until opposite the point where a small tributary stream runs in on the far bank (true R). Cross the river here. In the angle formed by the tributary and main streams a path leads off under plane trees, keeping close to the true L bank of the tributary. You come first to a patch of open 'fields', which you leave on your L, then to the Stavropogì-Mandrinì road (it doesn't yet connect up). Turn R - you are close to the river bank among firs - and cross a second stream (48 mins). Approximately 100 metres along on the L a path winds up the hillside through thick fir woods.

Cast about carefully to find the path; it is a long, long detour by the road. The path was obviously a major thoroughfare not long ago, but has fallen into disuse in recent years. There are plenty of clues to the line of the path. Its surface is stony and the roots that cross it are bare of bark, from the passage of feet and hooves. There are, however, places where it has been completely overgrown by broom and you have to push your way through or find a way round. You are in fact ascending the flank of a spur, and the best guide to direction is the ridge-line of the spur. The path winds up close to it, sometimes on it, sometimes to the R, but never L. There is a deepening gully on the L.

After 15 minutes or so climbing you catch a glimpse of the houses of Livadáki on a wooded spur to your L (1 hr 5 mins). About 10 minutes later you are on a level with Livadáki. There are remains of cultivated terraces in the gully on your L. The path here turns R away from the ridge of the spur.

Another 15 minutes (1 hr 20 mins) bring you to the chapel of Áyios Yánnis in a clump of fir trees at the top of the spur. To R and L are the remains of fields. Ten families lived here until the Second War, fled during the civil war and never returned. In 40 years nature has removed all trace of their houses.

There are walnut and plane trees in the 'fields' on the R; it is their lighter green foliage which makes a mark on the hillside visible from Mandrini. Looking back you can just make out the houses of Mandrini.

Beyond Áyios Yánnis the path is much clearer because of the traffic between Stavropigi and the chapel. As before, the path continues along the edge of the L hand gully. 15 minutes beyond the chapel (1 hr 35 mins) it bears away R. There is a bit of a wall on the R and more 'fields'. 5 minutes later you pass through a small V-shaped cutting with a slight rise in the ground to your R (1 hr 40 mins). This is the end of the ascent. Beyond this point the path bears L, with a ravine dropping away on the R.

At 1 hr 45 mins you reach the church of Áyios Sotíras standing in a walled cemetery surrounded by chestnut trees. At the corner of the cemetery you meet the road from Livadaki, and turn R downhill into the rather bare and severe-looking village of Stavropigi, formerly Ámbliani.

Stavropigì to Stàvli

Walking time: 2¼ hours

Stàvli is the nominative case and it is this which is found on the map. However, whenever you talk about where you are going or where you have come from, you use the accusative case: Stàvlous *(stàvloos)*.

There is a path which cuts over the ridge behind Stavropigì. I did not take it because of bad weather and because some old men who, incidentally, claimed to remember Lord Hunt passing this way in 1963, warned me that it was hard to find. Judging by the GSGS wartime maps, it seems to follow the telephone line, which is very probable - Greek paths often do. The modern 'road' to Stàvli swings west making for a natural gap in the ridge, now called the *dheeaklàdhosee melètsees* - the Melètsis crossroads.

Leave the *platèeya* and return along the road you arrived on. A path branches off R by a house 80 metres beyond the church. It climbs up through firs to the L of a shaly gully to meet the road again at 22 mins.

Turn R uphill. At 30 mins you come to a church on the ridge by a crossroads. A forestry track branches L. A little higher up, another road branches R for Gardìki, a village on the east side of Mt Saràndena. Keep straight on, that is, downhill and bearing L-handed. The road climbs steadily through thick fir forest until you reach the Melètsis crossroads at 55 mins.

Here you can see Stàvli to the north-west lying just under the ridge on the slopes of a steep bowl-shaped valley. Further off, beyond the ridge, the village of Krìkello appears, and further off still the conical peak of Mt Velòuhi and the peaks of Àgrafa.

Turn R at the crossroads. At first it is almost as if you are doubling back in the direction from which you have come, albeit on the other side of ridge. At 1 hr 17 mins, rounding a bend, you come in sight of Stàvli lying below you. From here the going is all downhill. At 1 hr 50 mins there is a spring by the road. At 2 hrs 5 mins there is a chapel on a flat spur sticking out below the road. The village is immediately below the spur with a path leading down from the chapel (2 hrs 10 mins).

Stàvli lies at about 1200 metres. It is pretty and derelict. There is a newly built *magazèe* and guest-house in the square. Facing you across the valley is the village of Dòmnista. The mountain blocking out the west is Kaliakòuda.

Stàvli has apparently always been known by this name. In ancient times, it was the seat of King Evrytas who gave his name to the county of Evrytania, whose borders you entered between Mandrini and Stavropigi - the poorest and remotest region of Greece.

I was told that after a long absence wolves have reappeared in the area, not in large numbers, but sufficient to harass the shepherds.

Stàvli to Krìkello

Walking time: 1¾ hours

Rejoin the road above the village, where a church stands in open grassy ground on top of the ridge. Turn L. After 50 metres a small track branches L from the road and continues along the top of the ridge. 100 metres later a path turns down R into the firs. The ground drops steeply away into the valley of the Krikellopòtamos river. Krìkello *(krèekelo)* is visible on a spur on the far side of the valley at roughly the same height as yourself. The path is fairly clear, but in places you are obliged to make considerable detours to avoid fallen trees which no one bothers to clear any more. The best guide is the telephone poles.

At 43 mins you hit the road, well down towards the bottom of the valley. Here you can play safe and follow the road into Krìkello. I ignored advice, tried to find the continuation of the path and got lost in a thunderstorm.

I could not find an obvious continuation of the path, but perhaps under pressure of the storm I did not look hard enough. Young firs obscure the ground on the opposite side of the road. I pushed through them into a patch of open grass and worked round to the R, where I found the path (45 mins) going in under the fir trees. Almost at once there is a stream. I made the mistake of going down the true R bank of the stream and was soon floundering about in soaking waist-high grass. I persisted in my error for a further ten minutes, during which time I stepped on the only deer I have ever seen in Greece. Uncertain how to proceed, I noticed the telephone line over to my R, struggled over to it and immediately found myself on the path.

So there is a 10-minute hiatus in the route here. The problem can probably be solved by a more careful search along the edge of the road. If it cannot, then keep to the R of the stream gully until you meet the telephone line. At worst you have only got ten minutes' anxiety!

At 1 hr 5 mins you come out on open ground above the river bank. A little way in front of you, upstream, is a three-log bridge with a handrail. Cross it and continue over the stony riverbed in a straight line from the bridge. Go through the stunted planes that grow along the further bank. Behind them is a patch of fields, at the back of which, almost directly in line with the bridge, is a well-used path that winds up the valley side through the trees. The trees thin out as the angle of the slope eases. You cross open ground, under a high tension cable, and into the lower limits of the village at 1 hr 45 min.

Krikello is a substantial village, the most substantial and prosperous since Åmfissa. It has a spacious treelined *platéeya* with a large stone church built in 1903. There are several shops and eating places, a post office, OTE and police station. There are daily buses to Karpenesí. It would make a good place for a day's rest.

Krikello to Karpenisi

Walking time: 5 hours

The dirt road climbs northwards out of Krikello up the thickly wooded west flank of the Krikellopótamos valley. The slopes below the road are covered with fertile, well-cultivated fields.

At 40 mins you pass a memorial on the R beside the road, dedicated to the memory of a doctor from Athens, who died at this spot in 1960 on his way back to his native village of Åmbliani. At 50 mins you come to a crossroads on the top of the ridge, with a hut on the R. Turn L for the village of Sigréllo *(seegrélo)*.

The Sigréllo track descends from the ridge in a north-westerly direction. At your feet is a broad amphitheatre. Over to the west you can make out the houses of Aniáda lying below a col to the north of Mt Kaliakoúda.

The track curves R through firs, then back L on to more open ground. At 1 hr 20 mins you pass under the telephone line. The poles march down into the valley bottom and up the opposite side to the top of a wooded ridge, behind which lies the village of Miríki *(meeréekee)* (due north). A path leaves the track at this point and follows the poles down into the valley bottom, where there are fields belonging to Sigréllo. This is the best way to go.

Following advice given me in Krikello, I went on to Sigréllo, a pretty but primitive village out of sight behind the two rocky hills to your L. The detour adds about 30 minutes.

To get to Sigréllo, just follow the track down to the river, through the narrow defile between the two hills and up a brief climb. To get back to your original line of march, take the path on the further bank of the river to the R. It brings you to the fields, where there is a junction of paths. The L-hand one leads round the uphill edge of the fields along the fringe of the woods to a stream gully in the topmost corner of the fields. The path goes into the stream bed, climbs out eight paces upstream and winds R-handed up through the trees until it meets the telephone line (2 hrs 25 mins) and the other path coming up from the R. (Note: the times given include this detour. If you take the direct route, subtract 30 minutes.)

Continue uphill across treeless ground towards the crown of the spur you are ascending. The path crosses to the L side of the spur and continues straight uphill with a deepening gully on your L. It is an excellent path, obviously a real highway in days gone by.

At 2 hrs 40 mins you emerge from the woods into open grassy ground with a clear skyline ahead. Keep straight up aiming for the telephone pole on the skyline. You pass a sheep-pen on the L. Continue upwards close to the poles over the open ground with a few scrubby bushes, until you reach the top of the ridge by a fir tree 20 paces to the R of the telephone line (2 hrs 48 mins).

A grassy track runs along the top of the ridge at right angles to the path. To the R is a wooded height with a building on the top that looks as if it might be an observatory or some military installation. Miriki is not yet in sight, but looking out over the woods in front you can see the houses of Karpenisi and Mt Velouhi behind it.

A little way ahead the telephone poles disappear from sight over a grassy edge. The path continues L of the poles down to this edge, whence Miriki is visible on the flank of a spur ahead of you. Down over open ground, the path enters the woods once more. There is a sizeable gully on the L and at first the path keeps close to its edge. At 3 hrs 2 mins the path turns R away from this gully, crosses a little stream beneath a plane tree, and shortly after there are the telephone poles again. Cross two more small streams running from boggy ground beneath plane trees, pass a patch of open ground enclosed by a fence on your L (3 hrs 9 mins) and at 3 hrs 13 mins you hit a forestry track by another stream. Turn L. There is a path on the L just below the track. Down across old fields, keeping R of the telephone line and L of the gully, the path leads to a bridge (3 hrs 37 mins) over a stream in the valley below Miriki. This narrow valley bottom is full of rich little fields, neatly hoed and manured and surrounded by jungles of vegetation, willows, planes, apple trees,

49

blackberries, and Old Man's Beard. Across the bridge a steep broad path leads to the *magazêe* in Miriki at 4 hrs 2 mins.

As you come out of Miriki, the road bends uphill to the R and a track goes off to the L. I went much too far to the R before making my way down L through the woods. According to the GSGS map the mule path clearly follows the telephone line, crossing a broad saddle before descending to the Karpenisiótiko river, which you should reach in not more than 40 minutes. Between the river and Karpenisi, which you can see just outside Miriki, keep to the R of the abrupt conical hill that rises out of the plain. Total time from Miriki should not much exceed one hour - i.e. 5 hours altogether.

Karpenisi, with a population of 4500 is a considerable town by Greek mountain standards, with several hotels and restaurants. Its setting is beautiful, on the edge of a small plateau ringed by mountains, with the 2315m Mt Velouhi *(veloohee)* at its back. (The view from the summit of Velouhi is great. The climb is easy but boring; the mountain is rather bare and there is a track all the way up, serving the rudimentary ski installations near the HAC refuge). The town itself is not much to look at. The Germans burnt it in war time and it was again fought over during the civil war, when the Greek communist guerrillas captured and held it for three weeks in 1949.

The bus station is on the top side of the central square. There are daily buses to and from Athens - about 7 hours - and connections on to many of the surrounding villages. The street that runs downhill from the L side of the square, as you face uphill, leads to another square where trucks that serve the outlying villages park. You can always get a ride on to the remotest places with one of these.

To get to the start of the next stage of the route, the simplest thing is to take take the bus to Kerasohóri *(kerasohóree)* (departure about 2 p.m. daily). It is a two-hour journey. You could walk it, but it is all road work - not that there is much traffic, and the scenery is spectacular. It would take all day. You follow the main road to Agrínio, which used to be dirt from Karpenisi on but is gradually being surfaced, cross the Mégdovas river and turn R for Víniani shortly afterwards.

KARPENISI to VRANGIANA

Scale 1: 200,000

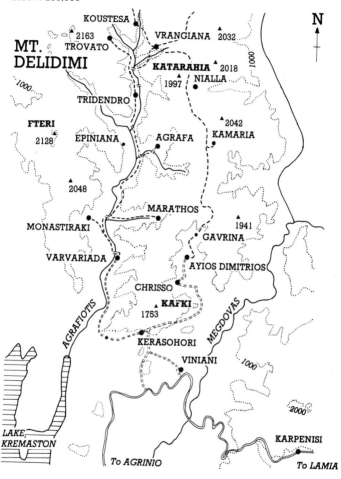

SECTION TWO: KARPENISI TO METSOVO

Maps: NSSG 1:200,000 sheets Evrytanias, Karditsis, Trikkalon
Total walking time: 53 or 58 hours

The country traversed in this section, though perhaps not as big and wild as that further north, is much the most difficult of access. The route followed is insulated from the outside world by a maze of lateral supporting ravines and ridges. And you won't get a square meal this side of Mètsovo!

(For access to Karpenìsi and Kerasohóri, the start of the route, see the end of the previous section .)

The first stage, from Kerasohóri to Vrangianà allows two alternative routes: one - the shorter - follows the beautiful gorge of the Agrafiòtis river. The other, via Àyios Dimìtrios and the Fidóskala or Snake's Ladder, involves a day-long ridge walk at about 1700 metres. The gorge is all enclosed, the ridge is airy. I'd say, do both!

Kerasohóri to Vrangrianà via Àyios Dimìtrios

Walking time: 15 hours

The dirt road to Àyios Dimìtrios *(àyeeos dheemèetreeyos)*, 4½ hours away, starts from the *platèeya* where the bus stops. Stand facing the little row of shops and shacks with the wooded peak of Kàfki rising to the north of the village. A rough track leads diagonally up to the R past the end of the shacks, where another track branches off L. Ignore it and keep R. For about 1 hour you follow the track, keeping more or less to the 900-metre contour just at the lower limit of the fir woods. To your R, the ground drops away into the wide valley of the river Mègdovas *(mègdovas)*, which together with the Agrafiòtis *(agrafyòtees)* and Aspropòtamos rivers drain the southern part of the Pindos range. Across the valley to the east rise the grey bulwarks of Mt Veloùhi.

At 1 hr the track bends sharply R and begins to lose height round a wooded spur jutting out eastwards. You could stick to the track. Better, there is a path on the L of this bend. Follow the telephone line through a small clump of firs. You emerge in a grassy field on top of the spur. Cross the field. There is no obvious path on the far side. Go down into the firs heading diagonally L. The slope decends steeply into a gully by the telephone poles. Aim for the poles. Scramble out of the gully into a meadow and the track is in front of you again (1 hr 13 mins). Turn L (north). Below the track on the R you look down on a group of three or four cottages almost buried in the woods at the edge of a clearing. They lie in a fold in the valley side, enclosed in silence so profound it is almost oppressive when you stop walking and the sounds of your movement cease.

On the far side of this depression the track curves L round a spur and you find yourself looking down over the valley of the Gavriniótikos *(gavreenyòteekos)* river, a tributary of the Mègdovas. Beside the road is a concrete memorial to men of Kerasohóri executed by the Italians during the war. From the memorial you look NNW up the valley to the peak of Prosiliakò *(proseelyakò)*, at whose foot lies the hamlet of Gàvrina *(gàvreena)*, though it is not visible from this point.

Beyond the memorial the track gradually loses height. Near the point where it comes closest to the Gàvriniótikos, at the foot of a rocky bluff, the river forks. The R branch leads to Àyios Dimìtrios and Gàvrina, while the L leads through a narrow defile to the village of Hrissò *(hreesò)*. The track follows the L branch into the defile. At 2 hrs 50 mins an old pack-horse bridge arches across to the further bank to link up with what appears to have once been a well-used path. 10 minutes further on there is a second bridge (3 hrs). Cross it and continue up the remains of the old cobbled way *(kalderèemee)*, which before long brings you to the track again. Turn R. At 3 hrs 30 mins you reach the edge of Hrissò.

At the lower limit of the village, the *kalderèemee* appears again and leads you into the centre. Its once neatly cobbled surface is all broken up. The walls that border it have collapsed and the once solid houses that stood behind them have crumbled to heaps of rubble overgrown with nettles and brambles. Hrissò, in fact, is fast being reclaimed by nature. A low whitewashed monastery church, apparently in good repair, survives just outside the village, but of the houses only a handful round the square remain intact and they are mostly boarded up. Despite the beauty of its setting Hrissò is one of the saddest and most desolate villages I have seen.

Beyond the village the track leads up over a low ridge and along the west flank of the Gavriniótikos valley to Àyios Dimìtrios in about 40 minutes (4 hrs 30 mins). Here by an old stone house on the L it comes to an end.

Just past this house, on the R, a leafy path leads down through lush fields to the *magazèe,* which stands in a little group of buildings with the church and school on flat ground in the valley bottom. This is the last shop before Vangrianå *(vranyanà),* though its stock does not amount to much. The man who runs it lives in the house where the road ends, mentioned above. It is as well to ask for him there, as the *magazee* is only open for limited periods. He will open up if asked. There are some good camping places on the way into the village.

From here to Vrangianå is 11¾ hours: 1½ to Gåvrina, 5½ to the shepherds' camp at Kamåria, another 1½ to the beautiful summer village of Niålla. Kamåria and Niålla make the best camping spots. Both have water.

A clear path leads north from the *magazèe* along the foot of the western side of the valley through lush vegetation, over streams, past scattered houses half-buried in greenery, to a bridge over the Gavriniôtikos. Across the bridge, the path climbs L-ward up the east flank of the valley to cross a wooded spur hiding Gåvrina *(gåvreena)* from view. On the shoulder of the spur (1 hr; 5 hrs 30 mins), where the path bears R into the ravine leading to Gåvrina, there is a chapel on the R and a circular stone-paved threshing-floor on the L. It is a magical spot. On the far side of the valley there are a few isolated houses in the middle of the woods, wild and remote.

The path continues through the woods along the R flank of the new valley, descending gradually towards the river. The peak of Prosiliakô *(proseeleeyakô)* and the rocky ridge behind Gåvrina are visible ahead. The path crosses the river - here no more than a boulder-filled stream - by a log bridge and enters Gåvrina (1 hr 30 mins; 6 hrs).

Gåvrina, entirely ringed by mountains, consists of two or three hovels with a few patches of maize. It is no surprise that when Lord Hunt passed this way in 1963 the people of Gåvrina said they had never seen a foreigner there before.

The path leads uphill out of Gåvrina. Just past the last house you cross a water conduit. I turned L here on the instructions of an elderly shepherd. Where you want to get to is the top of the ridge directly above the village. I was told afterwards that I should have turned R at the water conduit. So if there is anyone about, ask for the way to Kamåria *(kamårya).* If not, do as I did!

Turn L at the water conduit. The path crosses open stony ground, then curves R (1 hr 50 mins; 6 hrs 20 mins) up the side of a gully leading to the base of the conical peak of Prosiliakô. At 1 hr 55 mins

54

(6 hrs 25 mins) there is an oak tree standing on the near edge of a steep torrent bed. Turn uphill and R on a path that climbs steeply through the firs. At 2 hrs 20 mins (6 hrs 50 mins) you reach open ground. Bear L. At 2 hrs 30 mins (7 hrs) the path levels out along the slope under Prosiliakò. At 2 hrs 35 mins (7 hrs 5 mins) you come to a spring beneath huge plane trees. At 2 hrs 55 mins (7 hrs 25 mins) there are huts and a sheepfold on top of a jutting spur directly under Prosiliakò.

This is much further over to the L than you need to be, and there is no apparent way of proceeding. However, right behind the sheepfold is a steep rocky slope that has been fractured into thousands of little ledges and steps. A narrow goat path traverses across these rocks, working diagonally up to the R. In summer, follow the muddy marks and droppings left by the goats. The path will lead you back to the R end of the ridge in about 20 minutes.

After 10 minutes (3 hrs 5 mins; 7 hrs 35 mins) you rejoin the main path coming up over open ground much to the R of the route you have taken. At 3 hrs 15 mins (7 hrs 45 mins), after a short steep pitch, you clamber out on top of the ridge by a lone stunted fir. On the far side is a deep wooded ravine.

From the tree, the path runs up the line of the ridge, at first slightly L of it, then after 10 minutes crossing to the R. There is a hut in the bottom of the ravine to your R. Ahead is a stony gully leading to a low saddle connecting Prosiliakò to a grassy rounded height called Karagoùna *(karagòona)* on your R. You pass some broad slabs of rock that make a seat beside the path.

At 3 hrs 35 mins (8 hrs 5 mins) you reach the saddle, with a spectacular view across the deep valley of the Agrafiòtis river to the jagged peaks of Liàkoura and Ftèri on the western skyline. Below the saddle a gully leads down R to a spring, about 10 minutes distant. To your L is a wide grassy bowl on the northern slopes of Prosiliakò usually reserved for grazing cows and where in July masses of geranium macrorrhizum grow among the rocks.

From the saddle, the path turns 90 degrees R and continues northwards along the western flank of Karagoùna before dipping down and across a narrow turf-covered neck of ground with fir woods reaching up to the eastern edge. At 3 hrs 50 mins (8 hrs 20 mins) you come to a neat stone shepherd's hut and sheepfold *(stròonga)* shaded by firs on the narrowest part of the ridge.

Beyond the sheepfold the path climbs up a narrow rocky ridge to a reddish peak with a long drop to the east. There is disagreement about where exactly the Fidóskala, or Snake's Ladder, starts, but everyone appears to agree that this bit of the ridge at least is part of it. From the peak on, the ridge levels out, flat-topped and grassy, though not very wide, with superb views east and west. At the end of this level stretch (4 hrs 40 mins; 9 hrs 10 mins), the ridge dips into a broad saddle crossed by a shepherds' track that leads eastwards through the summer settlement of Kamària *(kamàrya)* to the village of Neràida *(neràeedha)* far below on the other side of the river Mègdovas. Another track winds up the north flank of the saddle and on along the ridge to the chapel of Áyios Nikólaos on the pass above Vrangianà. 20 minutes take you down to the track. There you turn down to the R across a pasture full of little streams. There is no point in following the track. You can see the Kamària cheesemaker's hut below you. The other huts lie just below that, 20 minutes from the saddle (5 hrs 20 mins; 9 hrs 50 mins).

Kamària is a collection of half a dozen tin-roofed huts grouped together round an enormous walnut tree on the otherwise treeless mountainside. It is a shepherds' summer camp. One of the huts has a fire-blackened stone embedded in the wall with the date 1872 inscribed on it, which is unusual in such impermanent dwellings. All the families who graze here are called Tsingarìdas and have probably been coming here for generations. A seventy-year-old granny said she had come every summer of her life. Her family winter at Livadià on the Athens-Delphi road and in the old days - up to the 1950's, that is - they used to make the journey to Kamària on foot with their flock, children and possessions: three weeks on the road twice a year.

There is a spring at the foot of the walnut tree and the remains of terraces where in former years they used to grow vegetables.

From Kamària it is about an hour's (1 hr; 10 hrs 50 mins) climb to the highest point of the ridge behind the settlement. Cross the ridge by the telephone line. There is an army fort, a ruined and primitive affair, built during the 1946-49 civil war in an attempt to control the movement of the guerrillas up and down the Pindos mountains.

From the fort, drop down to the track on the west side of the ridge and turn R. The track crosses a grassy amphitheatre and on the far side swings out west round a spur. Either follow the track round or cut up over the ridge. On the far side you look down into a vast and beautiful area of sloping pasture enclosed by two long projecting ridges. The northern one is dominated by the peak of Flitzàni *(fleedzånee)* (2018m). The continuation of your ridge is dominated by two peaks, first Katarahià *(katarahyà)* (1997m), below which lies Vrangianà, then Plàka (2013m). Lying well down in the pasture is the summer settlement of Niàlla *(nyàla)* with several old stone houses and a low slate-roofed church. Slightly to the north beneath the steep sides of Flitzàni is the smaller settlement of Péra Niàlla. A great place for camping and a good base for exploring.

Proceed north along the ridge past the foot of Katarahià. Just before you reach the red rocky ridge of Plàka, climb up the rounded slopes to your L (3 hrs; 11 hrs 50 mins). From the top you look over into a grassy cwm enclosed by the northern slopes of Katarahià with the ravine of the Vrangianà stream beyond. Vrangianà village lies on the flank of the ravine, but is as yet out of sight round to the L behind Katarahià.

Descend into the cwm. On your L is a steep crag with stunted trees hanging from its ledges, where choughs wheel. A stream gully - dry in summer - develops in the cwm. Follow down the R bank. As you come out of the cwm you see a sheepfold below, just R of the gully at the upper limit of the firs. The col at the head of the ravine to your R is where the old path - and now dirt road - from Vrangianà to Karitsa, Neohòri, Lake Tavropòs and ultimately Karditsa in the Thessalian plain passes over. Right on the col is the chapel of Àyios Nikòlaos.

From ridge to sheepfold is about 30 minutes (3 hrs 30 mins; 13 hrs 20 mins). There is a spring in the gully by the sheepfold.

From the sheepfold, a path crosses the gully and bends L round the base of Katarahià through the fir woods. The path is clear and follows the contour until you reach a point below the peak of Katarahià where there is a grassy clearing on a spur facing the scattered houses of Vrangianà on the far side of the intervening ravine. Be careful. This is the first clearing you come to. Do not go straight on, although there is a path. Turn very definitely R and go steeply down towards the bottom of the ravine. The path is clear and leads eventually to the first houses in the lowest quarter of Vrangianà (5 hrs; 14 hrs 50 mins).

Cross the river, which is full of water and very cold even in July, and head up the opposite side of the valley. The houses of Vrangianà are so scattered there are scarcely two together. There is a *magazèe* about half-way up the slope. The one I prefer is almost at the top, close to the saddle between Alogolívado, the wooded peak north of the village, and Psilórahi to the south-west.

The proprietor is Nikos Christou. He will always fix you a meal and provide something basic for the road. If need be, he will find an empty house for you to sleep in.

Though it seems incredible now, Vrangianà was home to some 3,000 souls in the 17th and 18th centuries, when its inaccessibility made it a favourite refuge of Greek patriots on the run from the Turkish authorities. A school flourished there - the teaching of Greek was banned in all areas under Turkish jurisdiction - and its church dates from that period.

The village would make a good base for exploring the surrounding peaks. Delidími *(deleedhèemee - 2164m),* the highest in the region, is just to the west, above the village of Trovàto.

The dirt road out to the north is of recent construction, and even now, in winter and bad weather, there is no way into Vrangianà except on foot.

If you want to leave the mountains here, you have to reach Neohóri *(neohóree)* before you can get a bus. In summer, you might get a lift; ask Nikos Christou. Otherwise it is five or six hours' walk. Take the old path rather than the road; it starts from the northern edge of the village, in the uphill corner and climbs the west flank of the ravine to the col by the chapel of Áyios Nikólaos *(àeeyos neekólaos)* - about 1½ hours. Thereafter, it is all downhill. On the far side of the col, where the road curves R, you can cut off a fair stretch by heading straight downhill into the gully below you, working downstream a few hundred metres, then climbing R back to the road by the Sarakatsan sheepfold at Krithària *(kreethàreeya).*

Kerasohóri to Vrangianà via Agrafiótis river gorge

Walking time: 10 hours

From Kerasohóri, follow the track westwards to the lip of the Agrafiótis river valley, ignoring the L turn into the village of Krèndi *(krèndee).* Once over the lip of the valley the track turns northwards and makes a long descent down to the river at the hamlet of Varvariàda *(varvareeyàdha)* (2 hrs 30 mins).

Varvariàda consists of a *magazèe* and three or four ruinous hovels shaded by giant planes and surrounded by lush riverside 'fields'. There is a spring. The sides of the valley close in here to form a narrow twisting gorge for the rest of the river's journey from its headwaters. Plane trees line the river-bed. The lower slopes are clothed in evergreen oak, which gives way above about 800 metres to the ubiquitous fir.

Just upstream of Varvariáda, there is a bridge. Cross over and turn R along a path that follows the true R bank of the river. Though it rises in places to 15 or 20 metres above the river-bed it never leaves the bank. 40 minutes from Varvariádha (3 hrs 10 mins) you pass Ayia Konstantína *(ayéeya konstandéena),* another tiny group of hovels beside the path, one of them serving as a *magazée.*

Continue upstream on the R bank. The river here sweeps R in a wide bend. A narrow ravine enters on your L. At its mouth you cross a bridge over a stream, on the far side of which is a tiny school-room for the few remaining children in the area. Just past the school, a path branching L up the R flank of the side ravine leads in 1 hour to the village of Monastiráki *(monasteerákee),* a beautiful but primitive village inhabited by only a handful of ancients. There is a path from here to Liákoura *(leeyákoora)* and Ftéri *(ftéree),* the peaks which dominate the western ridge of the Agrafiótis valley.

At 3 hrs 45 mins, rounding a bit of rocky cliff above the river, you come to the bridge of Karvasará, built in the 1960s to replace the old packhorse bridge which has collapsed. The path crosses over to the true L bank of the Agrafiótis at this point. Just below the bridge a tributary stream joins the Agrafiótis, flowing in from the east down another narrow wooded ravine from Marathós, a village just visible from Karvasará.

Karvasará - a corruption of *caravanserai* - consists of a handful of cottages scattered among the trees in the angle between the two streams.

Over the bridge the path turns L (north again) past an old stone cottage and climbs steadily uphill through woods of evergreen oak for the next 1½ hours. The path climbs to a considerable height above the river in order to get round the narrowest part of the gorge known as *ée tréepa* - The Hole. It is well-worn and easy to follow.

Numerous gullies scoured out by winter torrents cross the path. In exposed places, on cliffs and outcrops, the rock strata present violently contorted lines, often vertical and sharply folded back upon themselves like hairpins. Here and there on the western flanks of the gorge are isolated hermit-like cottages. This part of the gorge is dominated by the conical peak of Sára on the west bank.

At 4 hrs 20 mins, opposite the mouth of a long ravine on the west bank, the path makes a sharp R bend round a very noticeable rock pinnacle. At 5 hrs 7 mins, the ascent ends. A small path winds off R at the beginning of the descent. Ignore it. The main path keeps L and markedly downhill. You come to a roughly fenced enclosure where the path turns R and almost at once enters a grove of immense planes shading a walled spring (5 hrs 30 mins).

Thereafter, the path bears L-handed under the planes and follows a gully down to the boulders of the river-bed, where it turns R (north) and continues along the edge of the river among dwarf planes for two or three hundred metres before climbing once more up the east flank of the gorge. When you have reached a height of about 50 metres above the river, you can see ahead the point where another gorge comes in from the R. It leads to Àgrafa village. Away to the west are the bare peaks and ridges of Liàkoura and Ftèri.

At 5 hrs 58 mins there is a fork in the path. The upper branch leads to Àgrafa village in about 1 hour. It first follows the true L bank of the Àgrafa stream through a rocky defile, then crosses to the R by an old high-arched bridge. Over the bridge, turn R and you come to the foot of a dry gully. The main path was out of action the only time I visited Àgrafa, so I scrambled up the R flank of the gully in about 10 minutes and came out on top on a little plateau where the village stands. It is an attractive place and would make a good overnight stop. There is a fair weather track back to Kerasohòri.

For Vrangianà, take the lower path. In five minutes or so (6 hrs 5 mins), you cross the mouth of the Àgrafa stream by a modern bridge and bear L, once more following the true L bank of the Agrafiòtis. About 1000 metres up on the west bank lies the village of Epinianà *(epeeyanà)*.

At 6 hrs 38 mins you reach the confluence of the Agrafiòtis with the Aspròrema *(White Stream),* which flows out of a long ravine to the west. A few minutes later (6 hrs 43 mins) there is another bridge over the Agrafiòtis. Cross and turn R. The path now follows the true R (west) bank of the river. There are several beautiful shady pools which make idyllic bathing places.

In 40 minutes you reach Trìdendro *(trèedhendro)* (7 hrs 23 mins). The path passes the *magazèe,* and leads out of the village between houses and fenced gardens. Beyond the village it rises across a bare stony slope to a point about 30 metres above the river. Here, a path branches up to the L. Keep R and downhill, back towards the river.

The path winds among large planes. The gorge is much narrower now, the river too, its bed filled with huge spate-smoothed boulders.

Keep along the R (west) bank, ignoring the first bridge, a flat concrete structure which leads to the village of Valári *(valáree)*. At 8 hrs 8 mins there is a watermill and a cottage on the L of the path, occupied in summertime only, by an old couple who winter in Athens. 10 minutes later (8 hrs 18 mins) there is a second bridge, where the path divides. L leads to Trováto. The path for Vrangianá crosses the bridge and climbs up the R side of a very narrow and deep gully scoured out by the Vrangianá stream. It crosses L by a bridge and zigzags up a bare rocky slope. The gradient eases and the narrow cleft of the stream gives way to a more open valley, which in turn opens into the wide grassy amphitheatre where Vrangianá lies (9 hrs 30 mins). To reach Nikos Christou's *magazée,* bear L round to the top of the village..

Agrafa - looking out over Vrangiana village

VRANGIANA to MESOHORA : THE AGRAFA

Scale: 1:200,000

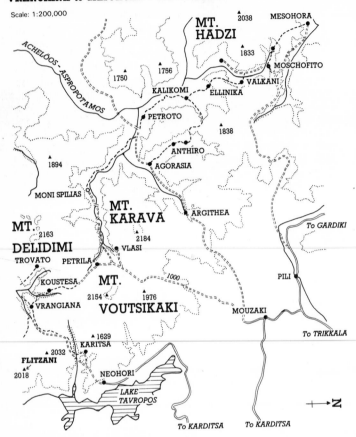

The road to Vrangiana

Vrangianà to Koustèsa

Walking time: 1 hour

The Koustèsa *(koostèsa)* path starts from the saddle above Nikos Christou's *magazèe*. In 1981, the first part of the path had already been bulldozed into a rough track, so it is not difficult to find. It descends due north down the east flank of the Agrafiòtis valley until it reaches the river.

After the first 20 minutes, you cross a stream below an isolated cottage. This used to be an idyllic spot, but bulldozer and avalanche have ripped out all the trees. After the short climb up to the cottage, the going is all downhill.

Cross the river where the path first touches the true L bank and strike uphill. It is best to make for the church.

Koustèsa to Petrila

Walking time: 4 hours

From the uphill edge of Koustèsa the path climbs steadily along the west flank of the valley towards the Agrafiòtis watershed, in fact aiming slightly L of the head of the valley. The woods are not continuous here. There is a spring after about 40 minutes (1 hr 40 mins). It is approximately 2 hours to the ridge from Koustèsa. On the ridge turn R on a rough track through open stands of fir. After some 15 minutes, the track descends the lower slopes on the western side of Mt Voutsikàki *(vootseekàkee)*. Keeping R of a deep-cut water-course, it leads to Petrila *(petrèela)* in 2 hours (4 hrs).

Petrila to the monastery of Spilià

Walking time: 3 hours

North of Petrila rises the vast bulk of Mt Karàva (2184m). At its foot, in a deep ravine, runs the river Petriliòtikos *(petreelyòteekos)*. About three hours' march to the west it swings north-west round the west flanks of Karàva to the village of Petrotò, where it joins the Aspropòtamos river.

About 30 minutes below Petrila you come to a crossroads, opposite and about the same altitude as the village of Vlàsi (vlàsee), which lies on the southern flank of Karàva. Turn L and follow the track along the southern flank of the Petriliòtikos ravine. As you round the bend into the first major re-entrant, a track leads down to an old stone bridge on your R - the path to Drossàto and Petrohòri.

Keep straight on, over a modern bridge and past a saw-mill.

At 1 hr 45 mins you pass the village of Paliohóri *(palyohôree)* on the L, at the entrance to a lateral valley running down off the northern slopes of Mt Delidîmi. Thence, the track winds down to a bridge over the Petriliótikos and continues west along the further bank. At the first bend, past an isolated house and *magazêe,* there is a small wayside shrine with a hut behind it. Turn L out of the track, round behind the hut and down into a rocky gully. There is no clear path; follow the telephone line. When you reach the river, turn R downstream under the trees until you come to another bridge. Ford the river and rejoin the track on the south bank.

The monastery of Spilià *(monêe speelyâs)* is now in sight, perched on the edge of a crag ahead of you. Follow the track until, rounding a last bend, you find yourself directly below the monastery. The track passes behind the monastery crag before zigzagging up the mountainside to enter the precinct from the west. There is also a path, which you can clearly see crossing the scree below the monastery buildings. Leave the track on this last bend (there is a cottage below on your R) and cut up the scrubby slope to the L. There is a spring at the top of the path on the L. You reach the monastery at about 3 hrs.

There are no monks any more, but in summertime there is a caretaker who will lodge and feed you (better not to count on it, though).

The site is spectacular. The old stone buildings - 17 or 18th century - sit atop a sheer-sided crag jutting out over the side of the Petriliótikos valley, hemmed in all around by steep wooded mountainsides. Low cells enclose the spacious inner courtyard, where a walnut-shaded fountain gushes icy spring water.

Spilià monastery to Petrotò

Walking time: 4 hours

There are two possibilities. One is to take the path from Stefánia along the west flank of the river valley, though I have been told by a local priest that it has collapsed in several places. The river, incidentally, changes its name to Koumbourianìtikos *(koombooryanèeteekos)* west of the monastery. The other is to follow the riverbed, which entails twenty or so fordings. This is the easiest route in normal conditions when the water is low; not so much fun, however, after a good storm. I did it after a long and violent night's thunderstorm, when the water was full of red mud, thigh-deep and fast - not an enjoyable experience when you are solo.

Looking west from the monastery you can see a very noticeable white hut at eye level about 1½ km away. Follow the track to it (20 mins), keeping straight on (L) at the only junction. At the hut, turn R off the track and down a path which winds down the west side of the wooded spur behind the hut into a cwm with a small lake. Mounds of moraine-like debris hold the lake back from spilling into the valley. The path peters out at the edge, but it is easy enough to clamber down R into the riverbed. Travel downstream (north) on the L bank.

The riverbed is wide, and both banks are lined with plane trees. The eastern (R) slopes of the valley - the flanks of Karàva - are thickly wooded to the top. The west are mostly bare. Riverbeds get hot in the middle of the day and the glare from the white stones is pretty uncomfortable. It is best to make an early start. The bulk of Karàva gives you shade until 10 a.m. or so.

The going is easy for a long stretch. There are signs of abandoned cultivation on the west bank and, high in the woods to the east, the occasional isolated cottage. There are occasional signs of life too -mule droppings, a flock of sheep. It is a lonely spot, and your sense of isolation is increased by not being able to hear anything but the sound of the river.

Past a deserted cottage opposite an unkempt grove of old olive trees, you are forced out on to the L bank to make a detour round some narrows. Soon afterwards begins the long series of fordings, inconvenient, but not the least hazardous in normal summer conditions. Eventually, you come to a confluence with a second river flowing in from the north-east. It is a beautiful spot where the two wooded gorges meet and all other sounds are shut out by the roar of the mingling waters.

Keep L at the confluence, following the L bank of the combined streams. The valley is more open here. High on the scrubby slopes to your R, you catch glimpses of the track from Petrotò to Argithèa *(aryeethèa)*. After three or four more fordings you come in sight of Petrotò on the R bank at a wide sweeping L-hand bend. Normally there should be no difficulty in getting out here. However, I found myself confronted by a lake of liquid mud filling the entire riverbed and was obliged to scramble out up the steep valley side to the Argithèa track.

Petrotó to Argithéa

Walking time: 5 hours

Only take this route if you want to get out of the mountains. It is 2 hours by the track to the hamlet of Agorasià *(agorasyà),* where there are a couple of *magazyà* by the road. The track up the valley to the north leads to Anthiró and Langàdi (see below).

It is another 3 hours to Argithéa, on the road all the way. It is easy walking, though uphill, up the valley marking the northern edge of Mt Karáva. The scenery is spectacular. There are several springs along the way.

Argithéa, tiny though it is, has something of a metropolitan air for the traveller off the mountains. It has electricity; the *magazée* even has television. It also sports the puritanical, but not uncommon, sign: 'Do not blaspheme against holy things!' It is beautifully situated in a green valley at the foot of the last barrier of mountains before the Thessalian plain. The track winds up over a high pass and down to Mouzàki *(moozàkee)* on the edge of the plain between Karditsa and Trìkkala. The region is frequently cut off in winter. There is no bus service, but you can easily cadge a lift on a truck. Ask at the *magazée* and, generally, they will arrange the lift for you.

Agorasià to Kalì Kòmi

Walking time: 3½ hours

(The best route to Kalì Kòmi *(kalèe kòmee)* is by the direct path from Petrotó - about 2 hours - on the east flank of the Aspropotamos or Ahelòós river valley. Through chance and circumstance I had to go via Agorasià and Anthiró).

Follow the track north from the Agorasià bridge up the west flank of the valley to Anthiró (1 hr). Continue through Anthiró on the same side of the valley to Langàdi (1 hr 20 mins).

Continue up the track for a further 15 minutes until you come to a patch of sloping meadow on the edge of a deep-scoured stream gully (1 hr 35 mins). On the further bank stand the much-restored barrack-like buildings of the monastery, Moni Kimiseos *(monèe keemèeseos).* Stand with the monastery on your R and face the ridge to the west. There is a line of firs on the ridge. The path to Kalì Komi crosses the ridge just L of the L-hand edge of the firs.

The meadow you are standing in is bounded by firs. The path begins in the uphill corner towards the edge of the gully. Through the trees - only a short distance - you come to a second meadow. Keep uphill close to the gully on your R and into the firs again. The way is not clear here. However, only a few paces higher up you come to a broad well-trodden path crossing your line of march. Turn R on this path, which crosses a stream and winds uphill through the woods. At 2 hrs 5 mins you emerge into a pasture of rough grass and bracken that continues up to the ridge. There are several paths and it is hard to decide which is the right one, though it does not really matter provided you keep working uphill towards the L-hand edge of the firs on the skyline. The path crosses the ridge at about 1300 metres between two boulders (2 hrs 50 mins). The view is superb on a clear day: you look south across the western slopes of Karàva to Delidìmi and the mountains of Àgrafa.

Over the ridge the path forks. Take the L branch. It runs along below the ridge for a few paces before dropping down into the woods, bearing R-handed. At the lower edge of the wood you come to steep, abandoned fields, bordered on either side by deep gullies whose streams converge at the lower end of the fields. The valley ahead of you opens at its further end into a broader one on whose western slopes you can see the houses of Ellinikà *(eleeneekà)*. Kali Komì is as yet out of sight to the L in this further valley. On your R, and slightly behind you now, is the peak of Zaharàhi (1838m), joined by a curving treeless ridge to Mavroràhi, the bare cone of rock diagonally to your R.

Go to the bottom end of the fields where they narrow to a point. There, in the midst of a clump of trees, you pick up the path again. It crosses the gully bordering the L side of the fields, then continues down the south side of the valley ahead of you. Half way down on the opposite side is the hamlet of Perivóli, a handful of whitewashed houses amid bright green fields - a minuscule oasis on the arid mountainside. The path continues straight across a patch of bare ground opposite Perivóli. Be careful not to take the R-hand path, which leads down to Perivóli. Thereafter, you begin to swing leftward into the Kali Komì valley. You reach the village after 3½ hours. The *magazèe* is next to the church, which you pass as you enter the village.

Kali Komì to Ellinikà

Walking time: 1½ hours

Go down to the river below the village and cross over by a log bridge on stone piles. Turn R and follow the bulldozed track as far as the first sharp L bend. There, by a red-roofed house, a path heads off R along a fence through scrubby bushes to the bank of a stream flowing down the west flank of the valley. Cross the stream and turn L up the further bank. It is stony going.

After a time the path leaves the bank of the stream and winds R past scattered cottages. The gradient increases as you gain height. Ellinikà *(eleeneekà)* is not in sight during the climb. The nearer you get to the village the clearer the path becomes.

Ellinikà to Valkàni

Walking time: 1¾ hours

Behind Ellinikà rises the bare stony height of Mavrovóuni (1278m). The path begins by a small chapel on the uphill edge of the village at the bottom L corner of Mavrovóuni and proceeds straight uphill to the ridge, keeping close to the base of Mavrovóuni all the way. Ignore the track.

On the ridge you rejoin the track and turn R, round the back of Mavrovóuni. At your feet is a deep valley with Mt Hadzi *(hadzèe)* rising to 2038 metres on the far side. The village you can see at its foot is Polynèri *(poleenèree)*. The dirt road running along the valley bottom leads to Moschófito *(moshòfeeto)*.

The track describes an almost exact semi-circle round the rim of a grassy bowl. At the far end of the curve, just before you enter the trees, turn down a path to the R. When you meet the track again, turn R and proceed to the first big R-hand bend, where the track loops right back on itself round a wooded spur. Just past the crown of the bend the path goes down the embankment to the L, chopping off the next hairpin and on to the track again. Cross straight over and down a well-used path slanting R through the trees. This is a beautiful stretch through tall stately firs, the ground underfoot soft with needles and forest loam. At 1 hr 30 mins, you rejoin the track towards the bottom of the valley. At 1 hr 45 mins, you reach the first, tumbledown houses of Valkàni. About 500 metres further on, turn L down a path leading towards the river and the centre of the village.

Valkàni to Moschófito

Walking time: 1¼ hours

Cross the river by the bridge just below the village. The track continues L. Take the path on the R which climbs the road bank just beyond the bridge. Rejoin the road and turn R for Moschófito *(moshófeeto)*. There is a *magazèe* on the R past the Moschófito bridge and a bus service to Mesohóra and Mouzáki.

Moschófito to Mesohóra

Walking time: 3½ hours

By the bridge, turn L up the track beside the river (true L bank). Past a small farm, the track curves L, pointing in the direction of a deep ravine coming down from the centre of the Hadzì massif. High above the point where this ravine joins the river, the track bends sharp R round a spur of rock. Spread out on the green hillside opposite are the houses of the nearly deserted hamlet of Stounári *(stoonàree)*. The track descends towards the river, which it crosses by a bridge just below Stounári (50 mins).

Over the bridge, there are some fields on the R by the riverside. A few paces beyond the bridge, turn R into a path that runs beside the first field. Climb the fence and cross the field towards the L. The river runs past the end of the field in a belt of planes. A little way upstream, the telephone line crosses the river. It is a vital landmark for most of the way to Mesohóra.

Wade the river and climb the opposite bank. The path at first keeps to the R of the telephone line, switches L, back again, and so on all the way up to the ridge ahead of you, without ever deviating more than a few metres either side, though in many places it is not very clear on the stony ground. The vegetation is open scrub and scattered oak trees.

About half-way to the ridge a kind of natural amphitheatre blocks the way. In front of it is a grassy plateau with broken terrace walls and other signs of former cultivation. The path makes a detour to the R keeping close to the R edge of the amphitheatre, then works back to rejoin the telephone line higher up. Close to the top of the ridge the oaks give way to firs.

At 1 hr 55 mins you reach level ground. In the clearings between the colossal firs are patches of grass full of flowers in spring time. The path goes through the belt of firs atop the ridge and emerges on the other side by a long stone drinking-trough. All around are green meadows running with water. To the north-east you can see the bald peak of Mt Avgò - *The Egg*.

Numerous small paths crisscross the meadows. The best thing is to follow the telephone line. Over a slight rise and down into a bit of a hollow, you come to a stream running off higher ground to the L, where a shepherd has constructed a sheep-pen out of interlacing branches and a small tree-house for himself in one of the trees. A little further on you cross a second stream in a stand of tall firs. Thence the path continues along the white shaly edge of a small embankment that faces eastwards over sloping meadows and fields. Ahead of you to the R a track ascends the hillside with an isolated house beside it. Keep along the top of the bank, through a stand of firs, over a patch of soft grassy ground to a shrine on a small saddle where the track peters out. From here you look out north and west to the Tzoumérka *(tsoomérka)* and Kakardítsa *(kakardhéetsa)* mountains with the Aspropótamos river at their feet. The village of Armatolikó is visible on the north bank. Immediately in front of you the ground falls away to a wide grassy bowl with a few scattered cottages and fields still in cultivation.

From the shrine, a rocky ridge projects northwards in the direction of Armatolikó. Mesohóra is out of sight below the northern end of this ridge. The path follows its western flank. Towards the end of the ridge it joins up with a much broader path coming down off the top. Turn down the new path and before long you come to a low wall and fence round a thick stand of trees - the upper limit of Mesohóra. Turn R along the path that skirts the wall and you arrive in Mesohóra by the offices of OTE at 3 hrs 15 mins.

Mesohóra is a large and relatively prosperous village, spread over a slope that faces north up the valley of the Aspropótamos. It even has a small hotel, and a bus service to Pýli *(péelee)* on the edge of the Thessalian plain.

Mesohóra to Gardíki

Walking time: 6 hours

The general direction is plain enough: simply proceed north up the Aspropótamos until you reach the first confluence in the west bank. There you turn south-west into a narrow ravine leading to Gardíki. The map marks a red road all the way, but I found only a forest track that would have been quite impassable for any vehicle other than a bulldozer.

In the middle of Mesohóra, just past the OTE office, turn R down a track towards the Vathírema *(vathéerema)* river which borders the east side of the village. You pass the hotel on the L. The track becomes a grassy path between scattered houses. Cross the grass in

71

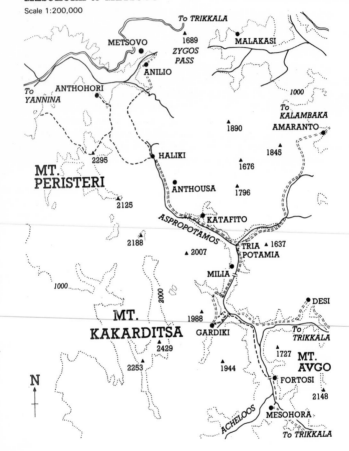

MESOHORA to METSOVO

Scale 1:200,000

To TRIKKALA

METSOVO

▲ 1689
ZYGOS PASS

MALAKASI

ANILIO

ANTHOHORI

To YANNINA

1000

To KALAMBAKA

AMARANTO

▲ 1890

HALIKI

▲ 1845

MT. PERISTERI

2295

▲ 1676

ANTHOUSA

▲ 1796

▲ 2125

KATAFITO

ASPROPOTAMOS

▲ 2188

TRIA POTAMIA ▲ 1637

▲ 2007

MILIA

DESI

1000

2000

MT. KAKARDITSA

1988

GARDIKI

To TRIKKALA

▲ 2429

▲ 1727

MT. AVGO

▲ 2253

▲ 1944

FORTOSI

N ↑

▲ 2148

ACHELOOS

MESOHORA

To TRIKKALA

72

front of the last house on the R and turn down a narrow path to the R which brings you to a concrete bridge over the Vathìrema. Cross and turn L through the plane trees on the further bank. The path emerges from the trees and climbs a little way up the bank, over-looking the junction of the Vathìrema with the Aspropótamos, where the collision of the two streams creates a great dimpled whirlpool. Goodness knows why the Aspropótamos is called 'white'; its waters are really a startling green!

Beyond this confluence the path drops to the water's edge and continues along the true L bank of the Aspropótamos to the hamlet of Fortósi *(fortôsee)* - just half a dozen cottages grouped round a fertile patch of alluvial deposit.

There is a broad sweep of pebbles and gravel on the Fortósi side of the river, while the current hugs the western bank. Close to the water's edge is a solitary tree with a very precarious-looking log bridge suspended on wires from its branches. Wooden steps mount to the main structure, which consists of three logs bound together and overlapping in the middle of the span with three other logs projecting from the further bank. There is a low uneven handrail. And as soon as you set foot on the bridge, the whole structure twists, bounces and sways, threatening to tip you sideways into the race of green water below.

Cross the bridge and turn R along the water's edge. It hardly seems as if there is a path at all. Pass a spring and then cut up a steepish bank through scattered oak trees to come out on the track from Armatolikò. (You can see it from Fortósi before you cross the river). Turn R on the track. There is a chapel in a clump of trees and a shack on the R of the track (2 hrs 50 mins).

Round the L-hand bend in the track ahead of you, a gully cuts back into the valley-side with houses on both sides. Either continue round by the track or cut down the path by the first house into the bottom, where there is a bridge over the stream, and up the steep further bank on to the track again, opposite the point where you left it.

Hereafter, you follow the west bank of the Aspropótamos, through thick oak woods. Approaching the junction with the Gardìki river the track draws nearer to the Aspropótamos. You realise how much height you have gained by the presence of fir trees right down to the water's edge.

When you reach the junction turn L towards the mouth of the

Summer pastures

ravine from which the stream issues. Cross the stream by a wooden bridge and turn L on the remains of a *kaldereemee* leading into the jaws of the ravine. At the foot of the cliff which encloses the northern side of the ravine, the *kaldereemee* peters out, obliterated by rubble from the track that has been constructed above it. Scramble up to the track and continue up it, cutting off the corners wherever possible. It is a stiff climb, particularly at the end of the day. You can see the telephone line to Gardíki crossing the slopes above you. It takes about 1 hour from the river to reach the road into Gardíki. Once on it turn L and in a few minutes you enter the village (6 hrs).

Gardíki is a big village, its substantial grey stone houses widely spread over the steep mountainside. It would make a good base for exploring the surrounding mountains, especially the area northwards towards Mt Peristéri, which looks very interesting. Mt Kakardítsa (2469m) is directly behind the village.

Though it fills up with native sons in summer, only a couple of dozen people stay through the winter. There are shops and a *magazèe* on the square. Don't be surprised if you hear a language that doesn't sound in the least like Greek. You haven't inadvertently crossed into Albania. Gardíki is a Vlach village.

Gardìki to Katàfito

Walking time: 4¼ hours

Leave Gardíki by road heading north, but do not turn down into the ravine you came up by. Keep straight along behind the rocky height that dominates the mouth of the ravine to the point where the road begins to descend. There is a shrine on the R, where you get a view away to the north up the valley of the Aspropótamos. The river is visible in the bottom, and some way upstream, in the woods on the west bank, you can make out the houses of Milià *(meelyà),* another Vlach village.

Beside the shrine a good path turns down R across a fir-clad slope in the direction of the river. You pass first through open woodland and across a rather barren slope of scree. Then the gradient steepens and the path winds down through denser wood to emerge on a gravelly bank a few feet above the river's edge. Walk a little way upstream to where a track crosses a patch of level scrubby ground to the water's edge (50 mins). The river is wide here, describing a broad, gentle bend. The valley sides have closed in to form a narrow, thickly wooded gorge with the fir trees growing right down to the banks.

Continue upstream along the lower edge of a boulder-strewn slope until you come to a junction with a tributary stream flowing in on the L. Here you rejoin the road and cross the tributary by a Bailey bridge. Not far up the tributary, out of sight behind an intervening hill, lies the village of Àyia Paraskevì.

Continue up the Aspropótamos until you come to a second Bailey bridge, where you cross to the east bank. Proceed along the east bank, past Milià, whose houses are just visible in the woods, past a wide flat meadow on the R of the track (2 hrs 35 mins), until you come to the crossroads at Tría Potàmia (3 hrs 15 mins) *(trèeya potàmya - Three Rivers),* where the Aspropótamos is joined by a tributary from the north-east. The R-hand track eventually leads out of the mountains to Kalabàka, by the monasteries of Metèora. The L (signposted Katàfito 5km, Halìki 16km) continues along the east bank of the Aspropótamos, which here changes course to the north-west.

75

Take the Halíki track. Katáfito is an hour away (4 hrs 15 mins), just a few minutes' walk up a side valley to the R. It, too, is a Vlach village, consisting of a few squat stone houses either side of a stream. It is remote and primitive. There is a *magazée* and the bus calls two or three times a week.

I spent the night in the home of a seventy-year-old widower, which I will describe to give some idea of the atmosphere in these villages.

It was a windy, snowy night in April. Vangeli's - my host's - cottage was squat and sturdy, with thick stone walls and stone slabs on the low-pitched roof. In front was a small vegetable garden. A hose-pipe brought water from a spring to a tap outside the door. There was a toilet in the garden, but no seat or flushing mechanism.

Inside the front door a passage ran the width of the house - it was only one room wide. There was no ceiling, just the smoke-blackened joists and rafters of rough-hewn pine. On the L, a door opened into a small low room where the old man lived. There was a fireplace where he propped fir branches against the wall, poured paraffin on them and got a fire going. The light was an oil lamp on a nail.

Vangeli's possessions consisted of two wooden beds, a rickety table, two chairs, a pair of heavy homespun trousers and an old jacket. The proudest piece was a battered Japanese transistor, a present from his son who lived in Athens, but he did not have any batteries and did not know how to change them.

Born in Katáfito, he had spent all his life there. He spoke with the usual mountain man's bitterness about neglect by successive governments. But it hardly mattered any more, he said; it was too late. Only a handful of old men and women were left waiting for the grave. He blamed the Forestry Commission for destroying the village's economy by banning the grazing of goats, sheep and cows in the woods. Livestock had been their livelihood, so everyone had been forced to sell up and go. And what was the point of the law? he asked. If sheep killed the trees, as they claimed, how had all those gigantic firs, years and years old, got there?

There was no arguing with experience like this. Vangeli had seen his world, a world that had existed for one thousand, two thousand years, destroyed in his own lifetime. Right or wrong, it is a loss as great or greater than the extinction of a species of flower or animal.

Katåfito to Halìki

Walking time: 2¼ hours

Walk back to the Aspropötamos and turn R up the track. It is a steady climb. The river twists and turns through a narrow gorge below the road, with lots of white water and clear pools. Here and there are patches of riverside meadow dotted with decaying farm buildings. Thick fir forest covers the mountainsides. There is a long beech wood on the ridge to your R just north of Katåfito.

The further you go, the wilder, steeper and lonelier the landscape becomes. Up the side gorges you catch glimpses of dark forest and high, snow-covered peaks and ridges. Firs with 60 to 80 feet of dead-straight trunk crowd in beside the road. There is no sound but your own feet and breathing.

Shortly before you reach the turning to Anthóusa *(anthóosa),* the next village north of Katåfito, you pass a tiny Byzantine monastery on a grassy mound on the far side of the river - Moni tis Panayås *(monée tees panaeeyås).*

The Anthóusa track goes off R along the edge of a stream gully on the edge of the woods. The houses are just visible through the trees about 1km away. Only two families winter there, I was told.

Cross the stream and carry on up the far side into a thick dark wood. Beset by spine-chilling thoughts of bear - they still exist in the area - I was glad to emerge on the other side in the wide grassy valley that leads up to Halìki *(halëekee).* The infant Aspropótamos is here no more than a little mountain stream tumbling down between grassy banks.

At the entrance to the village (2 hrs 15 mins), there is another attractive Byzantine church on the L - the monastery of Profìtis Ilìas. Cross the bridge and enter the village, which lies in the angle formed by the junction of the Aspropótamos with a stream that flows from the north-west off the slopes of Mt Peristèri (2295m) *(pereestèree).* It is a substantial village, totally deserted in winter and rather spooky. It, too, is Vlach.

Halìki to Mètsovo

Walking time: 4¼ hours

The track continues up the true R bank of the Aspropótamos, that is, up the R-hand valley as you face Halìki from the bridge. You can see it zigzagging up over the ridge at the head of the valley.

A short distance from the bridge it makes a long detour L into a re-entrant. At this point, cut down across the meadows on your R to the banks of the river, where there are remains of walled vegetable plots and several fountains. Continue upstream until the river divides at a spot known as Paliomonǎstiro - the old monastery, though there are no remains of any kind. The Aspropôtamos is the R-hand stream. Take the L, keeping to its true R bank. Ahead of you, a path crosses the stony slope below the rubble thrown down from the construction of the track. A little way along this path you come to another dividing of streams. The path crosses the L-hand stream and winds up the rocky ground separating the two, keeping rather towards the R branch. Zigzag steeply up. Coarse moorland grass has taken the place of the lush meadow. In places it is not clear whether you are following a path or a rain gully, but provided you aim for the track whose embankment you can see above you cannot get lost. When you hit the track, turn uphill. The view gets more spectacular the higher you go. You look way back down the Aspropôtamos valley over a long perspective of ridges and peaks.

Towards the Râhi Hôdza *(râhee hôdza)* ridge - the pass you are heading for - the track runs beside a funnel-like gully. Follow the old path up the gully as far as possible, then climb out on to the track. On a knoll to your L are two lonely beech trees, the highest for miles. In a high wind they make the most eerie screeching, audible long before you can see them.

At 1 hr 30 mins you reach the highest point of the pass at about 1800 metres. Far to the north-west you can see Mt Gamila *(gamêela)* towards the frontier with Albania. Leave the track, which goes off to the R here and peters out. Go straight on down the gully in front of you. You drop quickly down towards a wide expanse of mountain meadow known as *to mandrêe too hôdza,* Hôdza's sheepfold. At first, the path follows the R side of the gully below a bank of stunted beeches. Lower down, where the gully opens into the upper reaches of the meadow, it crosses to the L of a small stream and winds down in the general direction of a stone shepherd's hut located on the downhill edge of the meadow close to the upper limit of the fir forest. Enclosing the meadow to the west is a low ridge, to the east a stream gully, which gradually deepens into a considerable ravine debouching at its lower end into the river Rônas.

You reach the shepherd's hut at 2 hrs. The path begins again behind the hut and slightly to the R. It drops down into the firs, traverses L across a steep slope and comes out on the upper edge of

Mountain sheepfold

some grassy fields. Turn R along the upper edge of the fields before descending into the wood again and winding down into the bottom of the ravine which has its beginnings at the top of the Hodza meadow. When you hit the stream, turn downhill for a short distance until you come to a small log bridge. Cross over and continue down a well-trodden path past cottages and farm buildings to a concrete bridge over the Rónas. Cross the bridge and turn L up to the rough track whose ugly scar cuts across the bare contours of the slopes on the north side of the river. Turn L again on the track. The Rónas runs into the Metsovítikos river, a little way downstream from Mètsovo. High above the confluence of the two, your track bends R towards Anílio *(anéelyo),* Mètsovo's twin village, high on the southern flank of the Metsovítikos ravine, which you reach 1½ hours after leaving Hódza's meadow (3 hrs 30 mins). Mètsovo itself lies on the other side of the ravine. A good *kalderèemee* connects them, but it is a long haul down and up after a hard day (4 hrs 15 mins).

Mètsovo is something of a metropolis in mountain terms, and a considerable tourist attraction. It is very pretty. Its old houses have been well preserved, and its Vlach inhabitants still wear their traditional costumes. It is a bit artificial, though not obtrusively so. There are several hotels and places to eat.

Mètsovo has long been a prosperous centre of the Vlach wool and transport business. The weaving trade still flourishes, but in days gone by, when the Ottoman Turks ruled all the Balkans, the Vlachs traded their textiles way up to Bucharest and Prague and even into South Russia. They secured the freedom to do this as a concession from their Turkish overlords, largely thanks to Mètsovo's crucial strategic position astride the historic Zygòs (now Katàra) pass from Epirus to the plain of Thessaly. Julius Caesàr passed this way en route to his decisive battle with his rival Pompey at Farsala in 48 BC. There was a Turkish customs post on the pass until the First War, for it was only in 1913 that Mètsovo and Yànnina, Epirus's capital, became part of the Greek state.

There are daily buses to Trìkkala, Yànnina (often written Ioànnina), Thessalonika and Athens. There are also daily buses from Yànnina to Igoumenìtsa, the port for Corfu and Italy.

The dustcart

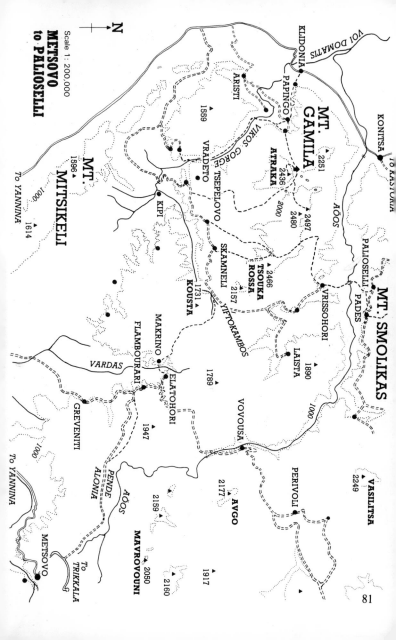

KLIDONIA

VOI DOMATIS

PAPINGO

ARISTI

1559 ▲

MT. GAMILA

KONITSA

To KASTORIA

VIKOS GORGE

VRADETO

ATRAKA

▲ 2251

2436 ▲

2497

2000

2480

AÖOS

PALIOSELLI PADES

MT. MITSIKELI

1596 ▲

TSEPELOVO

KIPI

To YANNINA

1614 ▲

1000

SKAMNELI

TSOUKA ROSSA

▲ 2466

MT. SMOLIKAS

2157 ▲

KOUSTA

1731 ▲

YIFTOKAMBOS

VRISSOHORI

MAKRINO

VARDAS

FLAMBOURARI

LAISTA

1890 ▲

1789 ▲

1000

GREVENITI

ELATOHORI

VOVOUSA

1000

1947 ▲

PERIVOLI

VASILITSA

2249 ▲

To YANNINA

1000

PENDE ALONIA

AÖOS

2177 ▲

AVGO

2159 ▲

1917 ▲

METSOVO

To TRIKKALA

MAVROVOUNI

2050 ▲

2160 ▲

▲

81

SECTION THREE: METSOVO TO MT GRAMOS

Maps: NSSG 1:200,000 sheets Ioanninon and Grevenon-Kozanis
Total walking time: 48 hours

This last section of the route is across heavily forested country, cut by two enormous ravines - Vîkos and Aöos - and dominated by three of Greece's highest mountains, Gamîla (2497), Smôlikas (2637) and Gråmos (2520m). Much of it is Vlach territory, both the villages and mountain pastures, though there is - or, rather, was - an important Sarakatsan enclave in the Zagóri, the area round the southern slopes of Mt Gamîla. It was this community that John Campbell wrote about in Honour, Family and Patronage (see Introduction/Books), a book now considered a classic of its kind.

The area used to be far more prosperous than it is now, as you can see from the surprisingly grand houses in villages like Tsepèlovo, Monodèndri and Påpingo and the churches in Samarîna and Läista. Like Mètsovo, they enjoyed various tax privileges under the Turks, until the rapacious and semi-independent Ali Pasha became ruler of Epirus in the late 18th century and grabbed everything for himself. He died in a hail of bullets on the little island in the lake at Yånnina, his capital, after a life of brutality and depravity. One of his most infamous deeds was drowning a gaggle of Greek girls in the lake, sewn up in sacks smeared with sugar, so legend has it, to make death sweeter. He also took a fancy to the young Lord Byron who visited his court in 1809, on account of his small ears!

The region suffered further through the second half of the 19th century, when it found itself on the wrong - i.e. Turkish - side of the northern frontier of the new Greek state and was consequently a frequent target of Greek nationalist raiding parties, for which the Turks took fierce reprisals. Local brigands did their share of the damage too, while the Romanians stirred up trouble among the Vlachs, arguing on the grounds of their linguistic affinities that they were really Romanians and not Greeks. Then, in this generation, war, civil war, and the general modernisation of Greece have all but completed the job of killing off these colourful and ancient communities.

Notwithstanding the sadness of .this, what is left is still very interesting, indeed unique in Europe. The scenery is superb, especially in the Aöos gorge. There are still a few bears. The shepherds see them occasionally. Wolves are relatively common, though a walker is not likely to see one. You might see a wild boar.

Some friends witnessed the amazing sight of a lammergeier lifting a tortoise into the air and dropping it on the road to break its shell. Flowers abound, in June and July especially - butterflies too. Gamîla and Smôlikas are noted botanical hunting grounds - Smôlikas, in particular, because its rock is serpentine rather than the usual limestone.

A word of warning: be extremely wary of the sheepdogs. Give them a wide berth wherever possible. They are trained to keep wolves, bear and intruders at bay, not to work sheep. They are always half-starved and won't think twice about making a meal of you. Carry a large stick - preferably, long and strong - and keep the brutes at a good distance. Never trust them, even when they appear to have been quieted by their master's command. You will be attacked several times a day, so be ready for it!

Mètsovo to Flambouràri and Elatohôri

Walking time: 8 hours

From Mètsovo village, walk up to the main Yánnina road and turn R up past the ski-lift to the beginning of the grassy plateau known as Politsiês *(poleetsyès),* where a track signposted Flambouràri *(flabooràree)* branches L across the meadow about 1 hr from Mètsovo. Flambouràri is 25km by the track.

The track follows the base of the wooded ridge enclosing the western edge of the meadows. The numerous springs and streams that make the area so green combine to form the river Aöos, which makes its way north, then west through deep forested gorges, to join the river Sarandáporos in the plain of Konitsa, whence the combined streams under the name of Vijose flow through the mountains of Albania to reach the Adriatic at Valona.

After about 1 hour (2 hrs) there is a spring at the edge of the woods on your L, followed 5 minutes later by a second, which pours its waters into a stone trough at the head of a little gully. Protected by a small spur projecting from the wood it makes an excellent camp site.

Continue along the track to the first crossroads, where a signpost says Dàsos Flambouràri straight on, Grevenîti and Flambouràri (18km) to the L. Turn L.

The track follows the R bank of a shallow stream between low grassy hills, past some fields and what from a distance look like ancient mine workings. Where the Grevenîti track branches L over a bridge and through a gap in the western ridge, keep straight on beside the stream until it bears away to the R. There the track climbs leftward towards the edge of a beech wood. Over the rise you come down to a R-hand bend where a path cuts straight ahead over a wooded shoulder. (You can just as well continue round by the track.) You find yourself on the rim of an enormous steep bowl, overlooking the valley of the Várdas river. Forests of Black Pine stretch as far as the eye can see.

Turn R along the rim of the bowl and into the wood. In a few moments you emerge on to open ground by two shepherds' huts (4 hrs). Beyond the huts the ground slopes gently down into a beautiful meadow dotted with stately pines. The track crosses the meadow to the L and disappears over the rim of the bowl into the valley below. The locality is known as Pènde Alònia *(pènde alònya)*.

From the huts, cross the meadow (straight ahead) to the edge of the woods on the far side. A grassy track goes into the woods at a slightly L-ward angle to your line of march. It is quite clear and is obviously occasionally used by forestry vehicles.

The woods are beautiful, the towering pines well-spaced, letting plenty of sunlight filter through to the forest floor which is thick with grass, bracken and box. There are masses of wild roses in July.

To your L the ground falls steeply away, affording long views westward to the long ridge of Mt Mitsikèli *(meetseekèlee),* behind which lies the city of Yànnina. The going is easy.

15 minutes (4 hrs 15 mins) from the Pènde Alònia meadow you come to a grassy clearing where there is a sort of junction. Keep L along the edge of the slope. 10 minutes later (4 hrs 30 mins) you pass a spring on the L. Another 8 minutes (4 hrs 38 mins) brings you to a stream, and up over a small rise to a fork in the path. Take the R branch which leads downhill. In 15 minutes (4 hrs 53 mins) you come to the edge of a huge landslip, where thousands of tons of rock and soil have fallen away from the side of a deep gully. You get a clear view over the eastern Zagòri to Mitsikèli and back to your L as far as Mt Peristèri. A further 10 minutes brings you to a spot where two streams cross the path, one tumbling from your R between large outcrops of rock. The purple flowers of the thistles which thrive in this moisture are a favourite haunt for butterflies, especially peacocks. And a colony of Butterwort *(pinguicola hirtiflora)* grows in the wet rocks.

20 minutes later (5 hrs 25 mins) you cross another stream. You are

84

Passing the time of day

walking on a forestry track here, overgrown but obviously used by vehicles periodically. After a further 20 minutes (5 hrs 46 mins), rounding a R-hand bend in the track, you get your first glimpse of Mt Gamila since crossing Hodza's Ridge south of Métsovo. 5 minutes later (5 hrs 51 mins), you come to the edge of a clearing and keep sharp round to the L.

At 6 hrs 5 mins quite a large stream crosses the track in the middle of a sharp L bend. On the R, in the trees, is the church of Ayía Paraskevi *(aéeya paraskevée)*. Just past the church, a concrete water conduit crosses the track, the water flowing L to R. The track to Flambourari continues downhill to the L. There is, however, a path, which I did not find. It apparently begins 100 metres downhill from the church and comes out three quarters of an hour later above the village. Worth trying, if you are feeling adventurous.

Otherwise, continue down the track, over a stream again, and keep L at the crossroads (about 6 hrs 10 mins). The gradient flattens out. In 5 minutes (6 hrs 15 mins) you come to an enormous clearing on the L with a small bungalow and telephone line. The area has been fenced off for use as a tree nursery. A little further, on the R, is a dilapidated children's holiday camp. You cross a bridge and a stretch of more open ground. Round the back of a long re-entrant, you begin to climb past abandoned terraces and orchards. The Greveníti road, which you join up with shortly, is visible below. At 7 hrs 20 mins you reach Flambourári.

There is a wooden *magazèe* in the square opposite the church, and a guesthouse - which I have not seen.

Another 50 minutes along the track, past the turning to Vovóusa *(vovóosa)* on the R, brings you to Elatohóri *(elatohóree)* (8 hrs 10 mins). The track ends in the square, overlooked by the *magazèe* on a small bump to the R.

Elatohóri perches on the slopes of a conical wooded peak called Tsoúka at the head of the Várdas river ravine. Like Flambourári, its tin-roofed houses have an air of weary desolation. There is a general lack of vitality about the place.

Just beyond the *platèeya,* down a broken cobbled alley, is a house that lets rooms. It belongs to the village entrepreneur, owner of bus and telephone. He has a loudspeaker rigged on a pole at his door which he uses to summon whoever is wanted on the phone. *'Còsta! Teelefono!'* rings out across the mountainside and five minutes later a stout little candidate for cardiac arrest appears mopping his brow out of the depths of the ravine. You can also get a meal here.

Elatohóri to Makríno

Walking time: 1 hour 20 minutes

Leave Elatohóri by the yellow house on the spur below the guesthouse. A path turns down to the R, signposted Läista - a village miles away to the north in the midst of the forest. It slants R-ward through cultivated plots, comes out on a bare gravelly slope, drops into a bottom at 15 mins, climbs to a spur at 28 mins and descends once more to a stream bed full of white boulders (44 mins). Cross the stream by a bridge of felled tree-trunks and walk a little way upstream. You can see the continuation of the path climbing back to the L on the opposite slope. At 50 mins you descend to a second stream between thickly wooded banks. On reaching the river bank, turn L, pushing through hazel bushes for a few paces, to a narrow hump-backed bridge. Then climb in a steady L-ward slant up the flank of the ravine through luxuriant vegetation to Makríno *(makrèeno)* (1 hr 20 mins).

You enter the village up a cobbled lane shaded by trellised vines, past a very pretty old church and campanile. The grassy *platèeya* is shaded by a giant plane. It is an altogether bewitching place, but has no food or accommodation.

Makrìno to Skamnéli

Walking time: 5¾ hours

A cobbled lane leads uphill from the *platèeya*. At the top of the village a well-trodden path turns up the L side of a deep little gully, following the line of the village water pipe. In 10 minutes you reach the top of this bit of ascent by an inspection cover for the water pipe. Beyond it the path bends R and at 20 mins you come to a track. Cross it and continue upwards. Great wooded valleys open either side of you. At 28 mins there is a fork in the path, where you take the L branch. You are ascending a narrow ridge between two valleys, the path at this point running just down to the L of the ridge line.

At 37 mins there are flat slabs of rock forming natural benches either side of the path, known as Àyios Kosmàs' benches. St.Kosmas was a zealous priest with a passion for learning and instruction, who toured the area in about 1775 preaching and founding schools. The Turks hanged him four years later. As proof of his eloquence and persuasiveness they cite the fact that the women of the Zagòri changed their hairstyles and headdresses at his order.

Up to this point the actual spine of the ridge has been bare of trees. From here on trees cover the whole ridge. At 50 mins the path crosses to the R of the ridge line, only to cross back a few minutes later. Thereafter, the pines thin out and for the last part of the climb the path winds up between stony, gritty banks to come out on a platform of level ground (1 hr 7 mins) where there is a shrine dedicated to Ayìa Marìna *(aèeya marèena)*. Beyond it is a forestry track. Turn R through woods of beech and pine. You are on the level here, even descending slightly.

At 1 hr 22 mins the track leads into a wide flat meadow. On the far side is a grey rocky bump covered with pines. Behind it to the R rises the peak of Kòusta (kòosta) (1731m), which dominates the area, A short distance into the meadow the track forks. Take the R branch.

There are some roofless shepherd huts in the meadow. It is a lovely place, marvellous for camping. (There is water).

The track re-enters the woods at the R edge of the meadow.

Hundreds of Loose-flowered Orchids grow there in June and July, whose tubers are powdered and used for making a thick syrupy drink called *salêpi*. You can sometimes find the drink on sale in the Omônia district of Athens. In Istanbul, in winter, it is a regular drink in the bazaars. It is very nourishing as well as being exotic.

At 1 hr 42 mins you pass a stream. Thereafter, the trees begin to press in more closely round the track. The Kôusta peak is on your L.

Many of the trees have huge wedges cut out of them - sometimes more than half the diameter of the trunk. This is because the wood from this part of the tree, called *dhadhêe,* used to be in great demand as a firelighter, a practice found in the Alps and Pyrenees too. It is prohibited today.

The track begins to wind up the L side of a gully to a narrow neck between two wooded ridges (2 hrs 2 mins). On the other side, it descends immediately with a deepening gully on the L. Go as far as the first R bend, and there, or just before, cut down L into the gully. At 2 hrs 12 mins you cross to the L bank of the gully. The stream itself is hidden from view by the massive leaves of the gunnera growing along its course. In 10 minutes (2 hrs 22 mins) you rejoin the track, here in pretty poor condition. Turn L. In another 10 minutes (2 hrs 32 mins) it comes to an end in a locality known as Pourniês *(poornyês).* Where the track ends, a shallow gully goes down to the R with the path beside it. Go steeply down through the firs to a grassy clearing (2 hrs 42 mins), whence you look over the tree-tops to the bare flanks of Tzoumâko, the most southerly peak of the Gamîla massif on the other side of the Skamneliôtikos river valley. There is a wild pear tree by a jumble of rocks in the middle of the clearing in front of you.

Take your time here, for the path is not easy to find. The obvious way ahead appears to be straight down past the pear tree to the bottom L corner of the clearing, where there is indeed a good path leading off L into the forest. However, do not go that way.

From the point where you first enter the clearing, go down diagonally R, leaving the group of rather scruffy trees in the middle on your L. The path you want leaves the clearing by the bottom R corner. The beginning of it has been obscured by young firs. However, if you continue a little way beyond the edge of the clearing you will pick it up clearly again.

You drop steadily down through open pine woods over rather gritty ground for 15 minutes until you come to a stream (2 hrs 57 mins). Cross it and turn L on a forestry track. A few paces (3 hrs) bring you to the junction with another stream flowing in from the R. Just beyond the confluence of the two streams your track joins another more used one.

This is another beautiful spot for camping and bathing, though mosquitoes are a nuisance at night.

Turn L at the junction of the tracks, down the R bank of the combined streams. 30 minutes bring you to the Skamneliòtikos river, whose deep ravine marks the southern boundary of Mt Gamìla. Just across the river the track joins the dirt road linking the villages of the western Zagòri with those of the Aòòs gorge. The riverside meadows here also make a good camp site.

(If you want to continue directly to Vrisohòri *(vreesohòree)*, turn R here. 40 minutes will take you to the open flat ground called Yiftòkambos *(yeeftòkambos)* (Gypsy Fields), where there is a roadside *magazèe* and a spring. A further 40 minutes (1 hr 20 mins) brings you to the Läista *(làeesta)* crossroads, where a Saraktsan family still builds a proper old-time hut of branches and there is a spring beside the road on the R. Keep L for Vrisohòri.

To your L thickly wooded slopes rise to the foot of the 1000-metre crags of Tsòuka Ròssa *(tsòoka ròsa)*, where patches of snow lie late in the year. To your R, the ground falls away to the great ravine of the Aòòs river, with the forested, rounded contours of Mt Smòlikas (2637m), Greece's second highest mountain, barring the northern skyline.

You pass several small streams in the first few minutes after the crossroads. Keep straight on again at the Iliohòri *(eelyohòree)* turning (about 2 hrs). At 2 hrs 35 mins there is a chapel on the R of the road and a spring, which is probably dry in midsummer. Thereafter, the track runs gently downhill through a lovely stretch of meadow dotted with walnut trees, until at 2 hrs 50 mins you come to a L bend with a culvert underneath. From this point you can see the pinnacle summits of Gamìla ahead of you and, over on your R, on the far side of the Aòòs ravine, the villages of Elefthero, Palioseli *(palyosèlee)* and Pàdes *(pàdhes)*. On your R, following the R bank of the stream that runs through the culvert, a good path leads down to Vrisohòri, whose roofs are visible below, in 15 minutes (3 hrs 5 mins.)

For Skamnèli and the other villages of the western Zagòri, turn L on the road, which follows the river at first, then parts company with

Shepherd's wife

it. Most of the way you are travelling through thick forest. Across the valley to your L, you look out at the rugged northern flanks of Kôusta, separated from its neighbouring peak, Kôziakas, by a wild wooded gorge. To the west of that are miles and miles of forested ridge and valley - bear and wolf country. It takes 2 hours to reach Skamnèli (5 hrs 45 mins). The *magazèe* is just off the road on the R.

Skamnèli/Tsepèlovo to Vrisohòri across Mt Gamìla

Walking time: 9 hours

This is an arduous but beautiful route, which takes you up to about 2200 metres. The descent is via the only weakness in the otherwise sheer defences of the north face of Gamìla. Indeed, this is the most spectacular part of the route, through thick beech and fir forest, with glorious views across the Aöös gorge to Mt Smôlikas. It is possible to do it in a day, if you start bright and early. No water for 5 hours, except the Goùra spring above Skamnèli.

Whether you start from Skamnèli or the neighbouring village, Tsepèlovo, the route is the same after the first 2½ hours. I would advise starting from Tsepèlovo, because the village is more interesting and because, that way, you can have the pleasure of meeting Alexis Gouris, who runs a *magazèe* on the little *platèeya* a short way up a cobbled lane on the R of the hairpin bend in the middle of the village. He has taught himself to speak English, is very charming and helpful, provides an excellent meal and will find you a room for the night.

Both routes are described - from Skamnèli, first.

Leave the village by the lane that leads straight uphill from the *magazèe*. Beyond the last houses it turns into a stony path, climbing steeply up the spur to the R of the big gully at whose bottom the village lies. At first, there are small terraced fields on the R, but higher up they give way to coarse moorland grass full of flowers. The path is clear, for it is in frequent use by the shepherds who pasture their flocks on the mountain above.

Once over the brow of the spur you find yourself at the beginning of a broad valley running north-north-west into the heart of the mountain, flanked on either side by steep rocky ridges. The ridge to your L is Kourtètsi, rising to 2169m at its northern end. On the R is the Goùra-Tsoùka ridge, rising to 2466m in the precipitous Tsoùka Rôsa peak. The valley floor is very uneven, dotted with boulders and broken by hummocks and outcrops. There are extensive limestone pavements, deeply fissured. There are masses of flowers: *doronicum*, *scrophularia* and ferns in the cracks in the pavement; clumps of sweet-scented *daphne oleoides* intermingled with violets, in the grass; *geranium subcaulescens;* campanulas, gentians, narcissus, saxifrages, and many others higher up.

There is no very obvious path, as the ground is criss-crossed with sheep trails. Head up the valley, keeping broadly to the R side. After about 1½ hours you come to a well-built stone hut standing a little above a grassy declivity with a concrete watering-trough and a brush-wood sheep shelter. The trough is fed by hose-pipe from the Goura spring which lies at the base of the sheer crag up ahead of you.

The valley narrows considerably beyond the sheepfold and the ground rises in the immediate foreground to an intermediate height below the Goura crags. When you get to the top of the rise you find a small cliff at your feet, which drops to an area of flat wet turf where the copious Goura spring rises (about 2¼ hours from Skamnèli). Above you on the L, the Kourtètsi ridge ends in a crag, at whose base a lower stony spur juts out like a prow, overlooking a large cirque. The back of the cirque is formed by a high wall of peaks, the highest of which is Tsoùka Ròsa. The way to Vrisohòri lies straight ahead up the curving wall of the cirque and over the little nick of a col close under the Tsoùka Ròsa ridge.

The deep-scoured valley running back west of Kourtètsi leads to Tsepèlovo, Skamnèli's neighbour to the west. The two routes link up on the floor of the cirque, in the locality known as *megàla leethàreeya* (see below).

If you are coming from Tsepèlovo, start in the *platèeya* with your back to Alexis Gouris's shop. Take the path which goes up to the R in front of you. It soon turns into a rough track going R-handed round the scrub-covered spur above the village, with a view back over the Skamneliòtikos valley. 20 minutes' walking brings you to a fork in the track by a walnut tree. Turn L, round the back of an intervening hill, then keep straight up the gully in front of you. The L side of the gully is defined by a line of cliffs, the R by the Kourtètsi ridge which separates it from the valley above Skamnèli (see above).

At 30 mins you pass a shepherd's hut and a grove of trees in the gully bottom, after which the gradient steepens. At 1 hr 5 mins, beneath a big cliff on the L, it levels off again. On your R are sloping pavements of fissured rock.

The path keeps R of a grassy hollow. At 1 hr 20 mins you are heading R-handed towards a ridge and cliffs, and in 5 minutes you come to a round pond with a paved bottom, for the sheep. Another few minutes (1 hr 30 mins) and the gully narrows; you start to climb towards a high V-shaped pass, which you reach in 30 minutes (2 hrs). Ahead of you are the great crags of the Goura-Tsouka ridge.

Cross the hollow beneath the L-hand cliffs, keeping over to the R (2 hrs 15 mins). Aim for the Goura-Tsouka cliffs. The Kourtetsi ridge on your R ends here. Keep R of the stony hummocks covering the valley floor. The locality is called *megàla leethàreeya,* after the huge boulders which dot the ground. The Goura valley from Skamnéli comes in here on your R (see above).

Walking parallel to the Tsouka ridge, aim for the col at the top of cirque above *megàla leethàreeya.* There is an obvious nick in the skyline. Don't cross the ridge to the R; there is a 1000-metre drop! The path zigzags up the col keeping to the R of the dry gully. It is not particularly clear, but it doesn't really matter. You reach the col at 3 hrs 30 mins.

Instead of the precipice you are expecting, there is a very steep scree slope leading to a long featureless valley full of grassy moraines. It is bounded to the west by a high ridge containing some of Gamila's highest peaks and to the east by the continuation of the Tsouka Rósa ridge, protecting you from the fearsome drop to the Aöös ravine. If you want to take a look at the drop, edge across the top of the scree to the R of the col, to where the ridge dips, enabling you to see out to the north. Vrisohóri is visible in the woods below.

The way ahead lies straight down the middle of the valley to a rocky little hill blocking the bottom. The path is not always clear. Aim first for the cairn on a hummock half-way down the valley (4 hrs 5 mins), then for the hill at the bottom (4 hrs 47 mins). There are cairns on the hill, and a sheepfold at its base.

Turn R at the base of the hill to go round it anti-clockwise. The trees begin again. You can see the village of Elefthero on the far side of the Aöös. In 30 minutes (5 hrs 17 mins) you reach a grassy bowl on the other side of the hill where a Saraktsan shepherd has his hut and a watering-place for his sheep. The locality is known as Kopàna.

As you look north towards Mt Smolikas, a steep gully drops away in front of you. The path down starts in the L corner of the bowl where you are standing (north-east) and winds down the steep grass and scree on the L side of the gully. After 30 minutes you pass a group of pines on the edge of the scree (5 hrs 47 mins). 25 minutes later (6 hrs 12 mins), towards the bottom of the treeless part of the gully, the path crosses to the R and soon after enters beech woods. Thereafter, it continues to lose height close to the R side of the deepening gully. At 6 hrs 30 mins there is a rocky clearing. The gully on the L is now very deep, the path traversing high among the pines which have now superseded the beeches. 7 minutes later (6 hrs 37 mins) you come to the end of the projecting spur forming the R flank of the gully you have been descending. The path bends R and in 20 minutes (6 hrs 57 mins) you come to a spring at the foot of a small cliff amid thick vegetation.

Beyond the spring the path climbs up into beech trees and again continues along the level to a second spring (7 hrs 17 mins). 15 minutes later (7 hrs 30 mins) you cross a grassy clearing on top of a rise, then descend among beech trees to a stream (7 hrs 35 mins). Cross two more streams, the second by an enormous boulder on the L (7 hrs 54 mins). Then up through a shaly gully to the R (8 hrs) and down across a clearing into beech trees. Across another clearing with scattered pines (8hrs 6 mins), losing height now. A few minutes later (8 hrs 10 mins) you come to the bank of a stream in the wood, where the path turns down to the L, crosses the stream, then turns downhill among beech trees again. A further 8 minutes (8 hrs 18 mins) bring you out on a forestry track at a sharp R bend. The tooth-like peak of Tsoúka Rósa is almost directly behind you.

Cross the track - don't go too far to the R - and go straight down into the pines. A moment later you come out on a bare shaly spur with Vrisohóri village in view below you. The path goes down the spur between two gullies, then crosses to the L, where they unite in a single deep gully. At the bottom of the descent the path crosses back to the R of the gully, rounds the end of the spur and crosses a bridge. At 8 hrs 40 mins you cross a second bridge and after a brief climb up a path overhung by hazel bushes you come to a chapel on the L - the beginning of Vrisohóri (9 hrs), a tiny, beautiful and nearly deserted village, barely holding its own against the enroaching woodland. There is a very basic *magazèe,* which can provide a meal of sorts. You will probably get accommodation in a deserted house if you ask.

Vrisohóri to Paliosèli

Walking time: 3 hours

The path begins by the monastery where a signpost points Pròs Yèfiran - to the bridge. At first, you go down a bulldozed track past a neat well-cared for cottage on the L with a garden full of flowers

and vegetables. In 10 minutes you come to a bend in the track (it peters out not far below) where a footpath strikes off to the R down beside a stream gully through a tunnel of hazel trees. The ground is wet with seepage and Marsh Orchids abound.

In 45 minutes you come to a high-arching packhorse bridge over the stream in the bottom of the gully. Overhung by trees and mossy rocks, it's a great place for a bathe.

Turn R over the bridge and in 10 minutes (55 mins) you pass a chapel with a pink-tiled roof. The path is clear, winding through thick woods of small scrubby trees: hazel, oak, ilex, beech and box. Here and there are patches of hay meadow, where butterflies drift and bask. After 1 hr 5 mins you come out on a ridge of friable, gravelly soil among oak trees, where you catch your first glimpse of the Aöös river far below. 20 minutes' descent brings you to an incongruous concrete bridge over the river (1 hr 25 mins).

There is a beach of brown gritty sand where the turquoise waters of the river slide by into the narrowest section of the gorge - good for camping, but no water handy.

The path turns L over the bridge and winds up through hot, tangy, resinous woods of huge Black Pine, with superb views back to the spectacular walls and pinnacles of the Gamìla massif. The path is easy to follow. 20 minutes above the bridge (1 hr 45 mins) there is an open grassy area beside the path on the R. At 1 hr 57 mins you bear L along an old retaining wall, keeping the wall on your R. At 2 hrs 10 mins there is a small stone shrine on the R *(eekòneesma)* and at 2 hrs 20 mins a pretty old chapel under an oak tree. A few seconds later you come to a fork: R for Pàdes *(pàdhes)*, L for Palioséli *(palyosèlee)*.

The path for Palioseli follows the R flank of a gully full of terraced fields. It is about 30 minutes' walk (2 hrs 55 mins).

Paliosèli lies on the dirt road connecting the villages on the south side of Mt. Smòlikas with the little market town of Kònitsa to the west. Like its neighbours, it is well-watered and green. Huge plane trees shade the *platèeya*. There is a *magazèe* on the road run by an old Vlach called Barba Mihos.

Paliosèli to summit of Mt Smòlikas (2637m)

Walking time: 6 hours

Opposite Barba Mihos's *magazèe* a cobbled lane leads to the top of

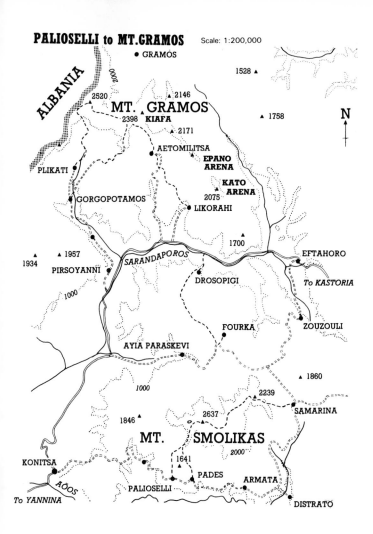

PALIOSELLI to MT.GRAMOS

Scale: 1:200,000

● GRAMOS

ALBANIA

1528 ▲

▲ 2146

MT. GRAMOS

2520

2398   **KIAFA**

▲ 2171

▲ 1758

N
↑

AETOMILITSA
●

▲ **EPANO ARENA**

PLIKATI

KATO ARENA

GORGOPOTAMOS
●

2075

● LIKORAHI

▲ 1700

▲ 1957

SARANDAPOROS

EFTAHORO
●

1934
▲

PIRSOYANNI

● DROSOPIGI

To KASTORIA

1000

FOURKA
●

ZOUZOULI
●

AYIA PARASKEVI

▲ 1860

1000

▲ 2239

1846 ▲

2637

● SAMARINA

MT. SMOLIKAS

2000

KONITSA
●

▲ 1641

AÓOS

● PADES

ARMATA

PALIOSELLI

To YANNINA

DISTRATO

the village, where to the L there is a small plateau full of fields watered by an irrigation channel coming down on the R. Behind these fields is a rocky bluff some hundreds of metres in length. Follow the path to the further (L) end of it, then head for the L-hand edge of a second rocky bluff higher up. The path climbs over shaly ground to the rim of a wide grassy plateau. At its inner, uphill, end is a copious spring marked by lush grass and ranks of Marsh Orchids. Bear R at the spring. The path bears R-handed through open woods of Black Pine and begins to work L-handed up the L side of a deep gully running down from the base of the summit cone. You cross numerous streams and patches of meadow. Be careful not to go too far over into the gully or you will have to make up the lost height later.

At the western edge of the summit cone you come to a broad shoulder at 2200 metres, with a small lake called, like its opposite number on Gamìla, Drakòlimni *(dhrakòlimnee)*. From here to the summit is a good hour's pull up steep shaly ground - of the one-step-forward, two-steps-back variety: not good for the temper. The view from the top, however, is stupendous, all down the Aöos gorge behind you and across to the cliffs of Gamìla, and away to Mt Gràmos in the north. It is probably best seen first thing in the morning, which means a night on the mountain. There are plenty of good camping places. You won't die of cold, but don't underestimate it. Drakòlimni has ice at its edges first thing, even in July.

There is a route off the mountain, due north from the lake, to the village of Àyia Paraskevì, which I have not done.

Smòlikas: summit to Samarìna

Walking time: 3¾ hours

The point to aim for initially is the rounded peak with the trig point at L end of the cirque beneath your feet. Go down the ridge at your feet and cross the narrow bridge of rock at the bottom of the slope (about 20 minutes). Continue along the now ascending ridge, but keeping to the R and below it, until you come to a tarn. Turn diagonally R down the gully which drains the tarn until you reach level ground by the ruins of a stone sheepfold. On your L is a big gap in the ridge-line. The route goes through this gap and down into the cirque. There is a yellow paint mark at the start of the path (38 mins). A few minutes later (45 mins) you pass a pool on the L fed by melt

The 'magazee'

water from a patch of snow that survives right through the summer. Follow the yellow paint splashes across the bottom of the cirque, then L-handed up a steep rock stair towards the top of the height with the trig point. Near the top there is a spring under a rock on the R of the path. Below, to the L, the ground drops away into a ravine leading down to the village of Áyia Paraskeví.

At 1 hr 20 mins you reach the top of the stair. Ahead of you stretches a broad, flat-topped ridge of reddish gravel with a line of small cairns descending diagonally R across it. In the middle distance, in front of you and slightly to the R, are two pointed wooded peaks. On your R the ground drops into another deep cirque. The route runs L of the rim of this cirque to its further end, where it traverses R beneath the two wooded peaks and crosses a saddle to the R of the second one.

Follow the cairns to the end of this ridge (1 hr 28 mins), where the path turns down a rocky couloir, levelling out at the bottom into a dry gully. Keep R of the gully.

At 1 hr 48 mins you leave a lone stunted pine on your R. Keep down L away from the rim of the cirque. In 15 minutes (2 hrs 3 mins) you come to the first trees, on the L. (You can see the white spot of the civil war memorial on Mt Gramos at 228° W.) The path passes L - handed round the back of a bump. 10 minutes further on you turn R to traverse across the face of the wooded peaks seen from the 'red ridge'. At 2 hrs 28 mins, turn up L by some big trees and over the col between Bogdàno peak on your L and Gorgòlu on your R. Samarìna village lies at the foot of Gorgòlu.

The path bears R as it crosses the col. At 2 hrs 38 mins there is a spring in a gully to the L of the path, known as Bogdàno. The trees hereabouts are Balkan Pines *(ròbola,* in Greek). A little further on the path crosses a second stream, then winds down R-handed into the trees.

At 2 hrs 58 mins you pass the Soupotìra spring *(soopotèera)* in a green, grassy clearing. Keep on down through the woods, until at 3 hrs 38 mins you emerge on to the bare slopes directly above Samarìna. Then it is only a few minutes down to the first building, the improbably large Samarìna hotel, built with the donations of Samarìna's emigré sons in the States.

Samarìna, once a major Vlach settlement with tens of thousands of sheep, is a semi-ruinous shadow of its former self. It was razed and deserted during the war and civil war. One of its nuttier inhabitants saw in the presence of the Axis powers an opportunity to set himself up as Prince of the Pindos!

The very fine church of *ste marèeya màre,* as it is called in Vlach - St.Mary the Grand - bears witness to the village's former grandeur, as do one or two semi-fortified houses and the monastery of Ayia Paraskevi *(aèeya paraskevèe)* about 40 minutes' walk down the track to the south of the village. The outside of the church is not much to look at, roofed as it now is in corrugated iron, but take a look at the painted interior - and the pine tree that grows from the roof of the apse and has been there as long as anyone can remember without getting any bigger.

Food and accommodation are no problem when the village is inhabited, from June to October. In winter it is snowbound and only a couple of people remain as caretakers. At 1600 metres it is the highest village in Greece.

The best time to visit, as it is with all the surrounding Vlach villages, is August 15, when there is a tremendous festival and Vlachs gather from all over Greece to celebrate.

Access is a problem, except on foot. A very rough, though

incredibly beautiful, track joins up with the Pàdes-Palioséli road to Kònitsa. The usual route is eastwards over the mountains to Grevenà, which has bus connections with Athens.

You'd probably get a lift in summer.

Samarìna to Mt Gràmos (2520m)

Walking time: 15 hours

The most satisfying conclusion, if you have done the whole hike from the Gulf of Corinth, is to continue on to Mt Gràmos on the Albanian frontier. The best route would be via Foùrka *(foòrka)* (2½ hours), Drosopigì *(dhrosopeeyèe)* (2½-3 hours), Likòrahi *(leekòrahee)* (2½ hours), Aetomilìtsa *(aetomeelèetsa)* (2½ hours) and on to the summit ridge by the civil war memorial. These times are rough estimates. I have not done the route, though I am sure it exists! It is marked on the old maps, and indeed on the current NSSG Ioanninon sheet - at least, there is a dotted red line running along the ridge from Foùrka to Drosopigì, which is definitely the line of the old mule trail.

The alternative is a long slog by the track - very beautiful, all down the deep valley on the north side of Smòlikas (2 hours to the Foùrka turning, another 4 - downhill - to the Kònitsa road); 1½ hours on the tarmac, followed by a good 4 hours up a track on the L to Voùrbiani *(voòrbyanee)*, Gorgopòtamos and Plikàti *(pleekàtee)*. It is very wild and sparsely populated country, thickly wooded and slightly spooky. They say there are still mine-fields in parts of the forest, from the civil war, when the Greek communists made this area their last stronghold. You can see why: ideal guerrilla country, especially before the roads were built.

The name Gràmos has immense emotive power over the Greek political imagination. For the Left it represents a heroic last stand against the forces of evil; for the Right, it symbolises the scheming wickedness of Bolshevism and especially of Greece's hated communist neighbours.

For these reasons, and lying as it does on the Iron Curtain frontier, Gràmos has been a no-go area for a long time. For many years you could not enter the area at all without a military pass. All this, to say that climbing Gràmos has to be handled with circumspection. Plenty of people do it. On the other hand, it is not clear whether you are allowed to. For Heaven's sake, don't try to get a permit. It will take a month of Sundays and the military will delight in saying no in the end. The best ploy is to be discreet and say nothing of your intentions to anyone. I did, and was promptly seen off by the tiny garrison stationed in Plikáti.

I got to the top by taking the track from Gorgopótamos, the village before Plikáti, to the civil war memorial. But it is a long haul, about 5 hours: 19km up the track and 1000 metres climb. Then another 2½ hours from the memorial west along the ridge to the summit, either via the military road built after the battle in 1949 or the crest of the ridge, which is covered with the remains of dugouts and bits of rusting metal. It is an amazing defensive site, well-nigh impregnable, surrounded on all sides by air. As a shepherd who had fought in the so-called Nationalist ranks told me: 'We could not get them out. It was the air force.' And they used US Helldivers, with US pilots, who tested the adhesive qualities of napalm on human flesh for the first time in combat. The summit, known simply as 2520 from its height, is a steep scree cone, from which you look down on the frontier following the crest of the north-south ridge just 100 metres below you. The Albanians patrol their side and you can see the odd machine-gun post. Just to the south are the ruins of the Greek fort where the Italians first crossed the border in their 1940 invasion, the beginning of Greece's involvement in the Second World War.

Beyond the frontier you look down into a deep and peaceful-looking valley with a ribbon of roads connecting a few small villages. In the distance there is nothing but mountains. It is curiously fascinating to stare down into this secretive little land!

Vlach shepherds on the Greek side said that the shepherds on the Albanian side - also Vlachs and some of them relatives - have not answered a *kalí méra* or accepted a cigarette since the revolution. 'Scared,' they say.

If you can evade the not very quick eyes of the military, much the simplest route is through the village of Plikati, down to the river, first on the true R bank, then the L, then the R again, where the ascent begins to steepen, leading to the ridge running north from Màvri Pétra *(màvree pètra)*, the great black crag behind the village. Walking time is around 4 hours.

And then you have to get down again, and back to the workaday world, which is not so easy! Aim for Kònitsa, which has daily buses back to Yànnina.

Olympus - the teeth of Mytikas. Photo: Alistair Scott

PART THREE

Shorter Walks:
One to Five Days

CENTRAL GREECE

OITI (2152m)

Map: NSSG 1:200,000 sheet Fthiotidos

Oiti *(èetee)* lies north of Ghiòna and Parnassòs, overlooking Lamìa and the bay of Thermopylae. The ascent routes are beautiful, both from the north and the south. The summit area, which is extensive, is grassy and undramatic, except in May when it is a mass of flowers - crocuses so thick you cannot help treading on them. The best hike is the complete traverse (9½ hours), which can easily be linked up with a traverse of Ghiòna or Vardòusia. A track connects Pyrà on the south side with Panourgià *(panooryà)*, whence there is a path to the Pyramìda peak of Ghiòna, and with Athanàsios Diàkos, the launching pad for Vardòusia.

Oiti is most easily accessible from the north. There are frequent buses from Athens to Lamia, and thence to Ipàti *(eepàtee)*, where the path starts. The train journey from Athens is fun, too; Lianoklàdi *(leeyanoklàdhee)* is the stop for Lamìa. It is famous for *reezògalo,* a sort of rice pudding, which swarms of enthusiastic vendors try to sell to every passing train. The line passes all along the side of Parnassòs and Ghiòna, then threads its way through some amazing defiles and gorges on the east flank of Oiti, before emerging above the Spercheios valley on a precarious ledge of rock, from which you look out to see nowt but air! On the way, you cross the Gorgopòtamos viaduct which was blown up in November 1942 by a combined force of clandestine British saboteurs and various elements of the Greek Resistance movements, under the command of Chris Woodhouse. A mere lad of 25 then, he later became Tory MP for Oxford and a leading modern Greek scholar. The purpose of the sabotage was to disrupt German supplies to Rommel in North Africa, which came down that little track. It is a major date in Greek history, because it brought together for the first and last time two Resistance leaders, the communist Aris Velouhiotis and the Right-wing Zervas, whose antipathy and opposition to each other brought about the first armed clashes in what eventually became a full-blown civil war.

The pull up from Ipàti is very steep, almost sea level to 2000 metres over a very short distance. I have described the route from Pyrà *(peerà)* on the south side, where you start at about 1200 metres. Access is via Kaloskopì: easy enough as far as Bràlos on the Thebes-Lamia road, not so easy thereafter.

MT.OITI
To LAMIA
Scale 1: 200,000
N
IPATI
KASTANIA
GREVENO
2116
GORGO POTAMOS
PYRGOS
2152
1613
To LAMIA
1400
KATAVOTHRA
1638
1789
PYRA
PAVLIANI
To BRALOS
To KALOSKOPI

Pyrå to the summit

Walking time: 3½ hours

Looking north from the village you see a very obvious bald peak, called Pyrå, dominating the skyline. This, or a point just to the R of it is your first objective.

In the middle of the village, as you approach from Kaloskopì *(kaloskopèe)*, a lane turns uphill to the R and on to the grassy slopes behind. To the L are big rocky bluffs with a stream at their foot, where orchids abound in spring. At first, the path keeps close to the L bank of the stream, then gradually moves away over the damp meadows. After about 1 hr there is a prominent rock on the L, some ten metres high, standing between two streams. Bear R away from the rock (at an angle of 2 o'clock, when you are facing uphill), keeping close to the R bank of the R-hand stream. The path first bears to the R, then back to the L, through juniper and scrub, up rising ground along the side of a gully. Over the rise you continue upwards with a stand of firs on your L. Here are big colonies of violets and *orchis pallens* in springtime. Behind you is the Pyramìda peak of Mt Ghiòna.

105

At 1 hr 30 mins you hit a forest track and turn L. A few paces later, round a R-hand bend, turn off R into a meadow with giant firs. At the top of the meadow, turn L up the bank into the trees (1 hr 45 mins). The ground drops steeply away to the west (your L), affording spectacular views of the peaks of the Vardoúsia massif.

Through a short rocky gully, then over a rocky tree-covered spur on to a shoulder (2 hrs) with a steep drop to the L, you enter a wide meadow. From the bank at the top end you can see southwards to Mt Parnassós. The track on the far side of the valley to the east leads to the village of Pávliani *(pávleeyanee)*.

Leave the meadow by the top L corner, where a good path follows the rim of the steep gully to the L through big firs. Keep on up to the timberline. The bald Pyrá peak, visible from the village, is ahead of you to the L as you emerge from the trees. To the R is a smaller rocky bump. Aim between the two. From the skyline a higher peak appears in front of you across an intervening dip. Contrary to appearances, it is not the summit. The highest peak, Pýrgos *(péergos)*, is just the other side of it. If you don't feel like climbing the first peak, it is easy to skirt directly round to the R to Pýrgos (3 hrs 35 mins).

Pýrgos to HAC refuge

Walking time: 2¼ hours

North-east of Pýrgos and some way off across the intervening meadows lies the Grevenó peak (2116m) with the HAC refuge at its western edge, reached through a narrow defile on the far side of the furthest expanse of meadow. The route lies along the track on the far side of the valley in front of you, through the dark belt of trees in the middle distance and across the meadow beyond.

From the top of Pýrgos aim straight for the track, keeping along the ridge or slightly R of it. It takes about an hour (4 hrs 30 mins) to reach the track. Turn R and follow it for about 45 minutes (5 hrs 15 mins) to a crossroads with a signpost erected by the monastery of Agathónos, which lies on the north side of Oiti. 100 metres to the R is a copious spring called *ee vreèsee too kalóyeroo* (the Monk's spring) overlooking the head of a deep valley running out eastwards. It is a good camp site.

A little further along the track and over a fast-flowing stream, you come to the wide, open meadows which stretch away to the foot of the Grevenó peak. In May they are covered with crocuses.

At the next junction in the track, strike straight ahead across the grass to a small lone pine. Over a slight rounded rise, where large circular clumps of juniper hug the ground, you can see the beginning of the defile leading to the HAC refuge. A good-sized stream runs through it with a track beside it. Go down to the track and turn L through the defile. After a few moments the refuge comes in sight on the flat top of a rocky shoulder, where the stream turns R and plunges into a deep ravine below Grevenò. The locality is known as Tràpeza. You reach the refuge at 5 hrs 50 mins.

The flat ground round the refuge makes a good camp site too, though it is advisable to keep well away from the trees, which bear the too obvious signs of lightning scars. There is a spring below the refuge signposted in a rather inconclusive manner by an arrow on a tree.

HAC refuge to Ipàti

Walking time: 3¾ hours

From the refuge go back to the track and turn R. The old path seems to have been obliterated. The best thing is to continue on the track for about 30 minutes, until you come to a sign pointing R to Perdikòvrisi *(perdheekòvreesee - Partridge Spring)* (6 hrs 25 mins). If you carry straight on you will eventually come to the village of Kastanià *(kastanyà)*. The spring is about 80 metres from the sign. The path is marked with red discs on the trees, which show better, however, when you are going uphill.

Stand with your back to the spring and turn L at an angle of 10 o'clock. The path is well-defined. It winds down through the trees, aiming west (L) of the big spur which forms the west flank of the ravine below the refuge. Keep R at a fork. At 6 hrs 50 mins cross a gully and climb up to the western edge of a lovely tree-encircled meadow named Amaliòlakka *(amalyòlaka)* after modern Greece's first queen - another beautiful camp site. There is water 5 minutes down the path at the *amalyòvreesee* spring. The path keeps along the very edge of the meadow before turning down to the spring (6 hrs 55 mins).

Thereafter, it turns down L and along the R flank of a deep ravine (rocky outcrop above on your R). After about 25 minutes' descent (7 hrs 20 mins), you come to a place where the path crosses open, shaly, eroded ground and you can see ahead to the mouth of the ravine and the flat land in the bottom of the Spercheios river valley beyond.

107

Packhorse bridge

There appear to be several paths. Keep to the L. Thereafter it is plain sailing, down through trees with the ravine on your L till you come to a patch of meadow after about an hour (8 hrs 20 mins), and the path becomes unclear. In front of you is a ruined mill by a stream and plane tree. Aim for the building. The path in fact goes diagonally L, crosses a water channel and turns back R to the corner of the ruin, where there is a large red paint mark. Thereafter, a clear path leads into the firs on the R side of a wooded hillock which stands dividing the meadow. It runs in a deeply eroded gully until at 8 hrs 55 mins it comes out in the open below the firs with a view over the plain.

The path continues clear and stony, bearing R across the lower slopes of the mountain. You come out on a track by a water conduit and follow on down to the village of Ipàti *(eepàtee)*. You reach the first houses at 9 hrs 30 mins.

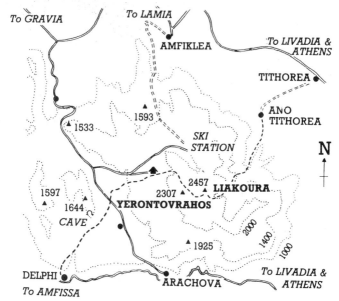

MT.PARNASSOS Scale: 1:200,000

PARNASSOS (2457m)

Map: NSSG 1: 200,000 sheet Viotias or Fokidos

The chances are, if you go to Greece, you will go to Delphi (hotels; several buses daily from Athens), which lies on the southern slopes of Parnassós. So it is a conveniently accessible mountain, if you do not have time for longer expeditions. It is also temptingly close to the pretty seaside village of Galaxidi *(galakseêdhee)*.

There are, however, some drawbacks, if this is to be your only mountain experience in Greece. Parnassós has become a popular ski-resort in recent years and has lost its virginity in consequence! Tarmac roads lead into the heart of the mountain, and people have begun to construct weekend chalets. It is also rather dull on the Delphi side - at least the 4-hour hike from the HAC refuge to the summit is. When the guide books talk about ascending Parnassós, it is usually this bit they are referring to. Forget it!

If you want to bag the summit, do it from Àno Tithorèa, or Velìtsa

109

(veléetsa), as the village is still usually called, on the east side of the mountain. It is an arduous but spectacularly beautiful route. If you have to start from the Delphi side, I would recommend two possibilities - one, part of the other: either a complete traverse of the mountain from Delphi to Velítsa via the HAC refuge and the summit (some 14 hours walking time), or, just the Delphi to the refuge stage (about 6 hours.)

Delphi to HAC refuge

Walking time: 6 hours

Note: when people mention Delphi in Greek you will later hear them say *dhelfóos*. This is because you use the accusative case when talking about going to and from a place. It is, however, the same place!

As you come into Delphi from the east (the Athens side), the road divides. Turn up the hill to the R. At the top of the slope turn R again on a lane that doubles back R to a house that once belonged to Angelos Sikelianos, one of Greece's best modern poets, just outside the perimeter fence of the archaeological site. There is a bust of the poet in front of the house.

Climb up the bank by the fence, through some almond trees, and follow the fence to its highest point. At the top L corner of the site, a cobbled mule path *(kaldeéeemee)* begins, zigzagging up the slope in long reaches. There is a fine view behind you of the olive groves of Itéa, the Gulf of Corinth and the mountains of the Peloponnese beyond (Zíria and Helmós).

At the end of the first R-ward zigzag you are directly above ancient Delphi. If you clamber out on the rocks, you look vertically down on to the ancient theatre. After 1 hour you reach the end of the *kaldeéeemee* by a large concrete inspection cover for the water pipe carrying spring water down to Delphi. You can hear the water banging hollowly about underground.

Turn L up the gully in front of you towards the heart of the mountains. The water conduit runs beside the path. After 1 hr 40 mins you come to a spring and watering troughs, with shepherds' huts scattered under the trees round about. Climb the low rise behind the spring and follow the track to the R. You very soon enter thick fir forest. I camped in the forest one cold December night, but there are better sites a little further on.

At about 2 hrs 30 mins you emerge on the other side of the forest. You can see ahead of you the rounded mass of the Yerondòvrahos peak (2367m), which guards the south-eastern approaches to Parnassòs.

At 2 hrs 45 mins there is a spring on the R, and a chapel and lean-to on the L, with a patch of grass in front that would make a good camp site. Past the chapel, on the R, is a muddy tarn backed by a low wooded ridge. On your L is a much bigger and steeper ridge on whose flank lies the ancient Corycian cave. Ahead of you lies a sizeable plateau, farmed by the villagers of Arahova, Delphi's eastern neighbour. As you move out into the flat fields on the plateau you can see the position of the cave high on the stony slope to your L. It would take about half-an-hour to scramble up to it; there is a track passable for vehicles, but it entails a fair detour to your L. The cave has very ancient associations; it was sacred to Pan and the nymphs, but there really is not much to see.

The tarmac road to the Parnassòs ski installations runs across the far side of the plateau. The low stone cottages by the road ahead of you comprise the summer village of Àno Aràhova, now only used for tools and livestock. Some way L of these old houses is a scattering of modern buildings near a bridge. Instead of following the track round to the L, strike out across the fields aiming for this bridge. Right behind it, is a narrow wooded defile.

You reach the road at about 3 hrs 40 mins. Cross over beside the bridge and start up the track on the true L bank of the gully. After 100 metres it crosses the gully, and one branch leads up to a modern taverna, where you can get refreshments and food.

Behind this building, two fir-clad bluffs stand either side of the defile mentioned above. Go down to the bank of the stream and across a patch of meadow. At its further edge a gully begins, its flanks badly eroded and carved out of a friable, gritty red rock. The path starts from the corner of the meadow and is marked by rusty red discs on the trees. For the first few paces it is clear, passing between small trees. Subsequently, it disappears. However, if you keep fairly close to the true R bank of the stream, you will pick it up again in a few minutes.

At 4 hrs there is a spring on the L. Thereafter, the trees thicken and you are soon in the woods again. After about 10 minutes (4 hrs 10 mins), you come to the edge of a steep scree-filled clearing where the path becomes faint. Keep up the L edge of the scree and into the trees in the top L corner. Keep straight up till you come out on a low saddle by a rusting sign (4 hrs 20 mins) pointing the way to the HAC refuge. Turn diagonally R up a stony slope, with trees on your R. Once over the brow of this rise and into the woods again the path is perfectly clear.

You are now travelling at right angles to your line of march before the saddle. The path sticks more or less to the contour, losing height slightly as you proceed. Yerondòvrahos looms ahead.

The path eventually joins the stream in the bottom of the defile to your R, crosses to the true L bank for a few hundred metres before returning to the R bank and emerging into a large open meadow encircled by trees, where it peters out (5 hrs).

On entering the meadow turn uphill to the L along the L edge of the meadow. Through some trees, into the open again, you come to a very rough track by an old well. Follow the track up to the Athens Ski Club road (5 hrs 25 mins). Turn R and either continue up the road or cut across country (diagonally R uphill). It is about 20 minutes to the HAC refuge (5 hrs 45 mins).

Refuge to Liàkoura *(leeyakoora)* (2457m)

Walking time: 3-4 hours

A few minutes beyond the refuge you come to the Athens Ski Club buildings in a hollow at the foot of Yerondòvrahos. There is a water cistern for sheep nearby, otherwise nothing for several hours, unless you happen on a shepherd who can refill your water bottles.

The start of the path to Liàkoura is marked with red paint by the fourth pylon of the ski-lift which mounts the slope of the bare ridge in front of you. It bears first L, then R up over the ridge into the long stony valley that runs all along the north-east side of Yerondòvrahos. It is waymarked periodically by splashes of red paint and cairns of stones. It is dull work, and since I last went this way the valley has been scarred by extensions of the EOT ski-lift network. Just keep plugging uphill beneath the cliffs of Yerondòvrahos till you reach the head of the valley after about 2½ hours. The path bends L-ward and you come eventually to a small saddle, where you look out over another valley running down L (north-west) towards the EOT ski resort at Fteròlakka. There are some shepherds' huts in the pasture in the bottom and a rough track on the slope behind, which, to the L, leads to Fteròlakka - an easy escape route if the weather turns nasty. Turn up the track to the R towards a gap in the ridge, keeping an eye open for the paint splodges which mark the route to Liákoura, now above you on the L. The ascent is an easy 20 minute scramble more or less up the ridge-line. On a clear morning - especially after rain -you are supposed to be able to see Olympus to the north, the Aegean to the east, Ionian to the west, and way down into the Peloponnese to the south. Twice I have stood on the summit at dawn and seen nothing but cloud - *póosee,* they call it!

Liákoura to Áno Tithoréa/Velítsa

Walking time: 4 hours

Just up the track from the foot of Liákoura, you come to the gap in the ridge on your L. A short steep scramble takes you down into the hanging valley where the path to Velítsa begins.

For the remainder of the route, reverse the ascent described below.

Áno Tithoréa/Velítsa to Liákoura

Walking time: 6 hours

The road from Káto Tithoréa, which lies on the Thebes-Amfíklea road and the Athens-Thessaloníki railway, aims straight as a die for the base of the Parnassós crags, which rise abruptly out of the plain above Velítsa.

At the entrance to the village the road crosses a gully, on the near edge of which a track turns up L across fairly even scrub-covered ground in the direction of the big Velítsa ravine. There are one or two forks in the track. Aim more or less straight up towards the mouth of the ravine, keeping fairly close to the gully side. In about 40 minutes you come to what is in effect the beginning of the ravine. The track suddenly gains height in a series of zigzags, before setting off up the L flank of the ravine. Cut off the zigzags, and head up the track for 20 minutes until you come to a small chapel on the R (1 hr). You can camp here. I have actually slept in the chapel; as long as you leave no mess I do not think it matters.

Leave the track at the chapel and aim straight ahead, where you will find the path going into the trees at the edge of the clearing by an open water-channel. Thereafter, just keep up the path, through fir forest all the way, with tremendous views of the crags leading to the summits on your R. 1½ hours above the chapel (2 hrs 30 mins) you come out on a narrow neck whence you look out L over the Boeotian plain. Ahead of you, a prominent rocky peak appears to block the ravine. In fact, the ravine bears L at its base, and a long hanging valley leading to Liákoura passes in front of it to the R. The path continues up the L flank of the ravine to a point below this peak, where it crosses the stream by a spring known as Tsáres (3 hrs 20 mins). Head up the steep slope opposite, through scattered firs. After about 25 minutes' climbing, you pass some sheep-pens. A further 40 minutes bring you to a stone hut in the mouth of the hanging valley (4 hrs 25 mins).

Thereafter, just keep up the valley floor to the top R corner (about 1 hour - 5 hrs 30 mins), where you scramble up a steep boulder-strewn slope through a gap in the ridge and on to the Fteròlakka track (see above). Turn R and up the ridge to Liákoura (6 hrs).

Mountain village

PARNITHA (1413m)

Map: NSSG 1:200,000 sheet Attikis

What Pàrnitha *(pàrneetha)* or Mt Parnes, as it is sometimes called, lacks in height, it makes up for in beauty. It is densely forested and cut by the splendid Goùra ravine. It is big enough in extent to provide a number of good walks. It catches enough snow in winter to turn the landscape into the proverbial fairyland and add an edge of excitement to walking. Its flowers are beautiful, especially in April and early May, and include some of the mountain flora, like crocuses, squills and tulips, as well as the orchids, irises and ophrys of the *maquis*. Although there is a tarmac road to the Mt Parnes Hotel and a dirt road encompassing the whole summit area, it is little frequented and the few visitors are soon left behind. It is a real boon for the Athenian, whether resident or in transit, just an hour's bus ride from Odòs Soùrmeli *(sòormelee),* near Omònia (buses daily at 6.30 a.m. and 2 p.m.). Once up there in the forest, you would never guess that the seething, noisy, polluted city was so close at hand.

I have described nine routes, some substantial, some just linking passages.

Route 1:   Thrakomakedònes to HAC Bàphi refuge

Walking time: 2 hours
(Bus No. 60 from Odòs Soùrmeli.)

At the crossroads about 5km short of the *téléphérique* to the Mt Parnes Hotel, take Odòs Thrakomakedònon - straight on, if you are coming from Aharnès; R if you are coming from the Athens-Thessaloniki road. Just past a large police compound on the L, you come to a bridge on a L-hand bend. Take the first L after the bridge, and keep L all the way, up Odòs Thràkis to where the road ends beneath some cliffs marking the beginning of the Hoùni *(hòonee)* ravine, which cuts deeply into the mountain just north of the Mt Parnes Hotel, visible, like the sore thumb, on the edge of its crag from all over the Attic basin.

Go up the stony track at the end of the road. Almost at once it becomes a path, which turns down L into a dry streambed. Cross over and continue on the opposite bank. The path is well-trodden and tightly enclosed by scrubby bushes for most of the way. There is no danger of losing it.

The height on your L is called Mavrovoùni *(mavrovòonee).* On

115

your R the sides of the ravine are rockier and more precipitous and end in sheer cliffs. The general direction of the route is in a slow leftward curve up the ravine.

After a while the path crosses back to the true L bank of the stream, traverses obliquely up a steep slope through trees, comes out high above the stream, then drops down and crosses once more to the R bank, where it remains. There is a steep winding ascent immediately after this last crossing.

After about 45 minutes you come to a junction, with a signpost indicating Katàra-Mesanò Nerò-Mòla to the R. Keep straight on. 10 minutes later (1 hr) there is another fork. Keep R and follow the red discs on the trees. At 1 hr 5 mins, at the top of a rightward traverse up a sparsely vegetated slope, just as you re-enter the firs you get your first glimpse of the refuge high on a rocky spur straight ahead of you. 20 minutes later (1 hr 25 mins) you come down to the confluence of two small streams. A sign on a tree points L to Àyia Triàda *(àeeya treeyàdha)*. A second path branches R to Mola and Koromilià *(koromeelyà)*. Take the third, middle path up a scrubby spur. At the top (1 hr 45 mins) you meet a wide path going off L, which leads to the dirt ring road, close to the turning to the Mt Parnes Hotel, 10 minutes' walk from the Àyia Triàda bus stop. Turn R and walk down into the head of a gully. The path crosses over and climbs back R to the refuge (2 hrs).

The refuge serves meals and refreshments, and has beds. However, the regime changes from time to time and it is worth finding out from the HAC in Athens what times it is open and what non-members are entitled to. I once spent a cold night on the porch without a sleeping bag! There is water at the back of the building.

Route 2: Bàphi refuge to Mòla spring

Walking time: 1 hour

This walk takes you round the eastern end of the summit ridge to the north side of the mountain. The first part is on the road, the remainder on a marked path through woods of Greek fir.

Turn R out of the refuge car park and follow the road until you reach the second track on the R - about 20 minutes. Go down this track about 30 paces. On your L at the edge of the trees is a red arrow marking the start of the path. Thereafter, follow the red discs on the trees. Be careful in the first 5 minutes as the path is not very clear, especially where you come to an open grassy clearing. There is no

Packhorse bridge

sign and you assume the way must be straight on. You should, however, turn sharp L.

There are no further difficulties for about 35 minutes (55 mins) until you begin to descend towards the ring road (never far below you on the R) and the path loses its definition. Just keep going down in an oblique line across the slope. You pass a spring and come to some picnic places under the trees, marked by low whitewashed walls. Go on to the road and turn L for a few paces. The spring on the L is Môla. The chapel opposite is called Àyios Pètros (1 hr).

Route 3: Mòla to Skìpiza spring

Walking time: 1¼ hours

Continue along the road past the chapel. There is a stand of poplars on your L in a patch of grassy ground. Turn L behind the poplars and you see a well-trodden path ahead of you. Follow the path into the trees and up a steep narrow gully with rocky sides. The way is clear and well-marked with red discs. After about 15 minutes the gradient eases. At 20 mins you come to a junction with two other paths. L leads back to the refuge. Straight up leads to the military camp on the saddle between the peaks of Òrnio with the telecommunications tower and Karabòla with the radar domes. For Skìpiza turn R.

This section of the path is soft and fairly level. On a fine day you can see Mt Parnassôs to the north-west and Mt Dìrfi in Evvia to the north-east. A surprising amount of snow collects here in winter, but when it melts the ground is covered with crocuses, alpine squills, *corydalis solida* and *anemone blanda*.

At 55 mins the path turns uphill to the L, crosses the western end of the summit ridge (1 hr 5 mins) and begins to descend leftward to Skìpiza *(skèepeeza)* (1 hr 10 mins).

Three other paths start from Skìpiza. One goes straight downhill to the Plàtana spring and the ring road in about 20 minutes. Stand with your back to the spring; the path starts between two trees in front of you and slightly R. The other two are dealt with below.

Route 4: Skìpiza to Bàphi refuge

Walking time: 40 minutes

Stand with your back to the Skìpiza spring. The path to the refuge is on your L, setting off uphill at an angle of roughly 8 o'clock. It is

118

easy going and marked by red discs.

After the initial ascent the path levels off along the top of some rocky bluffs where a beautiful wild tulip grows in June - a good picnic spot with long views out over Elefsina and the bay of Salamis to the mountains along the north shore of the Peloponnese.

Out of the trees and across a series of eroded shaly gullies you come to a tarmac road (about 25 minutes). Turn L down to the ring road, which you reach in about 10 minutes. Turn L again and in a few paces you find yourself at the Báphi refuge car park (40 mins).

Route 5: Skìpiza to Àyia Triàda

Walking time: 1 hour

Stand with your back to the Skìpiza spring. The Àyia Triàda path is on your L at an angle of 10 o'clock. It is all downhill. There are no junctions.

Shortly after starting you cross a section of deeply eroded ground where the path itself turns into a stream after rain or when the snow is melting. On your L are the rocky bluffs along the top of which Route 4 passes. Thereafter, the path enters thick fir woods, crosses an eastward-rising slope into a well-defined valley that blends slowly rightward (southward) and brings you down a stream gully to the ring road a few paces uphill from the Paliohòri spring (45 mins).

(To find the path if you are going up to Skìpiza from Àyia Triàda, look out for the spring. It is on the R of the ring road just past the crown of a L-hand bend. Opposite is a very noticeable piece of flat ground with rows of ventilator pipes like pointed hats sticking up. The path goes up the stream which emerges beside the spring - about 15 minutes from Àyia Triàda).

For Àyia Triàda, turn L up the ring road. In about 15 minutes you come to the tarmac. Turn L and Àyia Triàda is right in front of you (1 hr). There is a spring and kiosk selling sweets and tobacco. This is where the bus stops (No. 64). There are only two a day back to Athens, at 8 a.m. and 4 p.m. Alternatively, you can walk to the Mount Parnes Hotel and take the *téléphérique* or walk back down Hòuni to Thrakomakedònes.

Route 6: Àyia Triàda to Thrakomakedònes via Houni

Walking time: 1½ hours

Continue along the ring road to the Mt Parnes Hotel turning, on the

R at the top of the first rise (10 mins). The ring road bends L here. On the bend is a signpost indicating the HAC Båphi refuge.

A few paces along the ring road a dirt track turns off R. Take it. Keep R at a junction - more or less a continuation of the direction you have been following. The track soon becomes a gravelly path winding between young fir trees down the R side of a gully. In a few minutes you come to the Kandàlia (*kandàlya*) spring with a flat-topped cistern behind it. Here the path forks. The L path leads to the Àyia Triàda-Mòla-Koromilià junction mentioned under Route 1, where you would turn R and descend Houni by the path ascended in Route 1. The R fork bends back to the R high up on the flank of the Hòuni ravine. It appears well-trodden at first, but quickly loses definition. Do not lose heart however. Follow it to the point where it peters out altogether, then cut straight downhill for about 40 metres until you intercept the main path described in Route 1.

Route 7: Àyia Triàda to Hasià

Walking time: 3¼ hours

(Bus No 64 from Odòs Soùrmeli to Àyia Triàda: two daily - 6.30 a.m. returning 8.00 a.m. and 2.00 p.m. returning 4.00 p.m.)

This walk takes you from the centre of the Pàrnitha massif to the village of Hasià (*hasyà*) - now officially called Phyle (*feelèe*) - at its southern end. The greater part of the route is along the east flank of the Goùra (*gòora*) ravine, which cleaves through the mountain in a south-westerly direction.

From Àyia Triàda go back along the road past the hotel, Ta Kiklàmina, then turn R up the so-called ring road. At the top of the rise, turn L down a forest track. (Do not take the footpath which branches L from the track.)

On your R the ground drops away to a grassy hollow which eventually develops into the Goùra ravine. On your L, a broad meadow lies at the foot of a low wooded ridge where the swath cut through the trees serves as a ski piste in winter.

As you proceed along the track the trees press in closely, shutting out the view. The going is more or less level. After about 40 minutes (40 mins) you come to a more open stretch where you can once more look out R over the Goùra ravine. The peak directly ahead is Kyrà (*keerà*). In early May the ground here is thick with orchids and irises.

Just beyond this open stretch, the track strikes the flank of Kyrà and turns sharply back R to follow the mountainside round. Conspicuous among the trees on the far side of the ravine to your R, at about the same altitude as yourself, is a villa with a red-tiled roof. It was built by the dictator Papadopoulos. At about 50 mins, just past the point where you are square on to this villa (a bald rocky bluff above you on the L), there is a concrete culvert under the track. 45 paces beyond the culvert on the R, a path descends into the bottom of the Goura ravine. Opposite (L), a small cairn marks the start of a path leading to the summit of Kyrà.

At the further end of Kyrà (1 hr), you come to a wide round space like a parking area. A track goes R into the ravine. For Hasià, keep straight on across the open space and out along another track on the other side. Where the track forks, take the R branch and five minutes after leaving the 'parking area' (1 hr 5 mins) you come to a yellow hut on the L. Go straight on into the low scrub beyond. 5 minutes later (1 hr 10 mins) the path comes to an end on the bank of another, very rough forest track. On to the track and turn R. You can see a rocky bump on the low ridge turning across right in front of you. Go down the track about 200 paces. On the R, on top of the earthy bank, a cairn marks the continuation of the path.

Up a grassy bank, through trees, round behind the rocky bump referred to above, you come to a junction with another path coming in from the R (1 hr 20 mins). You are on a flat, broad ridge. Take the R path. In 50 metres you come to another junction where you fork L. Be careful here.

The junction is marked by a cairn of stones. The path goes between some low bushes and down a gentle slope into the trees. If you stand at the junction and look down the line of this branch path you will see, in the middle distance - perhaps 1km away - the more or less conical top of a hill sticking up; the actual tip is bare rock, while the lower slopes are covered with firs.

Line up on this hilltop. The path from where you are standing to the open ground at the foot of this hill is marked with red discs. However, there are none at the start of the path (though there are small cairns) and thereafter there are several misleading goat trails. If you keep your eye on the hilltop ahead of you you cannot go far wrong. It is better, if anything, to err towards the R; straying too far L could land you in the wrong ravine.

15 minutes should bring you to open ground with obvious traces of farming activity (1 hr 35 mins). You can see the cliffs of Àrma to

your R (number of rock-climbing routes) on the far side of the Goùra ravine, which you here rejoin.

Aim for the opposite R corner of this open ground, where you will easily find the path again, running along the side of a slope facing the Goùra ravine. In 5 minutes (1 hr 40 mins) you reach the lip of the ravine. Climb down beneath a steep slope. A 10-minute descent brings you to a very attractive spring at the foot of a cliff (1 hr 50 mins). The water, which is channelled into hollowed pine trunks, runs all year round, creating a little oasis of freshness and greenery. Should you come on it, as I did once, on a hot summer's day, to find an old weather-beaten shepherd watering his flock, it is a truly bucolic spot. This particular old man had been born on Pàrnitha. His mother was out working in some poor stony fields beyond Àrma that used to be cultivated, when she felt her time come, and simply dropped her son on the path! A measure of how much things have changed in Greece in a single lifetime.

Beyond the spring the path climbs over a rocky shoulder and begins to descend through woods of Aleppo pine, whose trunks are scarred by resin-tapping. In 15 minutes (2 hrs 5 mins) you come to an open grassy meadow. Cross it and carry on down through the woods. The path has been worn down into a deep gully by the passage of men and mules. It is marked by red discs and splashes of paint.

20 minutes bring you to the bottom of the descent (2 hrs 25 mins) in the angle of a re-entrant, where a narrow gorge comes in from L. From here on, a broad level path follows the steep flank of the ravine. On your R, on the opposite side, the convent of Moni Kleistòn *(monèe kleestòn)* tucks in under the cliffs of Àrma.

In 3 or 4 minutes you come to a curious concrete construction in the middle of the path. Its form has been rounded and distorted by incrustations of calcite. It has a grill on top, through which it emits gurgling and sucking sounds. If incautiously you peer in to see what it is all about you are likely to receive a sudden squirt of water in the eye - rather refreshing on a hot day. It appears to be a sort of blowhole in the pipeline bringing spring water to Hasià.

Past this contraption the path develops into a lane, curving leftwards round the red crag that marks the southern end of the Goùra ravine. 15 minutes later (2 hrs 45 mins) you pass under the electricity cables, carried up the valley on pylons. Fields and olive groves appear here - a blaze of flowers in spring. Hasià is visible to the R ahead of you. 20 minutes beyond the power line you reach a tarmac road (3 hrs 5 mins). Turn R and in 10 minutes (3 hrs 15 mins) you come to the 'main' road in Hasià village opposite the bus stop for Athens.

Route 8: Àyia Triàda-Goùra-Pan's Cave

Walking time: 3 hours

Follow route 7 as far as the culvert opposite Papadopoulos's villa. Then turn down R into the bottom of the ravine. The path reaches the stream just downstream from the fence enclosing the so-called Pàrnitha game reserve. Turn L along the L bank of the stream. The way is marked. The path crosses back and forth over the stream several times until, eventually, you come out on a track (maybe 1½ hours from the culvert). Turn R and follow it down to where it crosses the stream (15 minutes). Turn L down the R bank of the stream for 5 or 6 minutes, then, where the stream gully opens out a bit, cross over and steeply up the L bank. The path is marked by cairns, but the stones are well lichened and do not show very clearly. About 10 minutes later, or just downstream from the confluence of two streams and about 20 metres above the water, you come to the cave. It is really a big overhang with a plane tree in front.

Route 9: Mòla-Malakàsa

Walking time: 3¼ hours

Take the track just past Mòla (see route 2) that turns down R into a large meadow. Follow the track L-handed across the meadow.

Do not take the R fork. Aim for the L corner of the meadow and the electricity cables. When the track peters out, follow the power lines to the R. Four electricity poles along, at the top of a rise, you come to a bit of stony, open ground, where the path is just discernible, crossing to the L side of the power lines. Go over a small gully, bearing leftwards away from the power lines. If you look back at the summit of Parnitha, you should be in line with the mid-point between the OTE telecommunications tower and the radar domes on Karabòla.

At 25 mins there is a red arrow on a juniper bush. On your L is a developing gully. The general direction is down the R flank of this gully. There is the odd cairn, but the path is faint on the stony ground and eventually peters out. Keep straight ahead down the flank of the gully. (Alternatively, go into the bottom of the gully and follow it down.)

At 45 mins you hit a track and keep straight along it, down into the gully referred to above (1 hr) and on along the L side of the gully. There are strawberry trees, pines and firs in the bottom here.

At 1 hr 25 mins you come to a place known as Koromilià *(koromeelyà),* after the wild plum trees. The track takes a 90 degree turn to the L. On the corner, a path goes R into the grass. There is a red arrow on a tree, pointing R to the very obvious gap between two heights, where the long ravine leading down to Malakàsa begins. The narrow defile between these heights is blocked by scrub. The path, clear but overgrown, passes through the defile on the L side of the gully. At 1 hr 45 mins you come to the narrowest part of the defile. In front of you a rocky shoulder forces the path down into the streambed. It follows the streambed for a short distance, then crosses on to the R bank. The path is clear.

At 2 hrs there is a grassy clearing and a second stream comes in from the R down the ravine up which the electricity lines pass. Cross to the L of the stream. At 2 hrs 12 mins you come to some tin huts in a clearing, and cross back R of the stream. At 2 hrs 20 mins there is another clearing. Climb up R over a bump, pass under the power lines, descend to a second stream, cross it and rejoin the main stream. The path becomes a track, which climbs up the R side of the gully away from the stream. At 2 hrs 28 mins pass under the power lines again and at 2 hrs 40 mins you come to a spring by some very big planes. 15 minutes later (2 hrs 55 mins) you reach the mouth of the ravine, with an army camp over on your L and a view of the Athens-Thessalonika road ahead. The track bends R and joins another track, where you turn L and continue on down to Malakàsa railway station (3 hrs 15 mins), where there are trains back to Athens.

EVVIA

DIRFI (1743m)

Map: NSSG 1:200,000 sheet Evvias

The sharply conical peak of Dirfi *(dheèrfee)*, rising from a long narrow backbone of high ground in the middle of Evvia *(èvya)*, is a prominent landmark for miles around. It is visible from Parnassòs, Pàrnitha, the Athens-Lamia road. The ascent is not specially interesting, but the views and the sense of airy elevation are exhilarating. It is conveniently close to Athens, not much more than two hours by car. There are buses and trains to Halkìda *(halkeedha)* and a local bus on to Stenì *(stenèe)*, at the foot of the mountain.

Stenì is a pretty village (hotel and tavernas) at the mouth of a wooded ravine leading up to the long Mesòrahi *(mesòrahee)* ridge connecting Dìrfi to the lower but more precipitous and interesting Xerovoùni to the south-east. There is a footpath leading up to the HAC refuge (about 2 hours) through fine woods of chestnut, beech

MTS. DIRFI and XEROVOUNI Scale 1:200,000

N

HILIADOU

▲ 836
LAMARI

MT. DIRFI ▲ 1743

STROBONES

1000

STENI
▲ 1417

MT. XEROVOUNI

To HALKIDA KAMBIA

EVVIA

and fir. There is also a dirt road, which has partly obliterated the path.

On the ridge there is a ramshackle snack-bar called *pàno apò ta sèenefa* - Above the Clouds. The refuge is 20 minutes north-west of it along a rough track, at the south-east corner of the peak. There is a spring nearby.

For the peak, continue past the refuge to the end of the track (10 minutes). A path drops into a hollow past a sheepfold. On the other side of a narrow neck of ground an HAC red arrow points upward - the start of a 2-hour slog right up the ridge-line to the flat craggy summit.

Other possibilities

From the *pàno apò ta sèenefa* snack-bar a very bumpy track leads down a lovely, wooded valley to the sea, via the villages of Stròbones and Làmari *làmaree)*. It is a good two hours by car, in second gear. It would be a long hike, but very lovely - and little frequented.

The track reaches the sea by a small river on one of the finest beaches I have seen in Greece, called Hiliadòu *(heelyadhòo)*. It used to be quite unknown, but no more. There is a taverna at the bottom of the track. You could still have it to yourself on a weekday outside July and August. In summer there is a bus to the beach from Stròbones, which in turn is served by a bus from Stenì.

OCHI (1349m)

Map: NSSG 1:200,000 sheet Evvias

Mt Òchi *(òhee)* lies behind the sleepy little port of Kàristos at the southern tip of Evvia. The area has not been much developed yet, and there is plenty of good swimming, so this can be a combined walking and lounging trip.

A simple ascent from Kàristos is not particularly interesting, as the mountain has been almost completely denuded. A complete traverse, however, over the summit and down the very beautiful Kallianòs *(kalyanòs)* ravine to the sea, where there is a remote and secluded cove, makes a very enjoyable and not too demanding walk. It is practicable most of the year.

There are daily ferries from Rafìna to Kàristos, and buses from Athens to Rafìna. The terminus is at Green Park, off Leofòros Alexàndros.

126

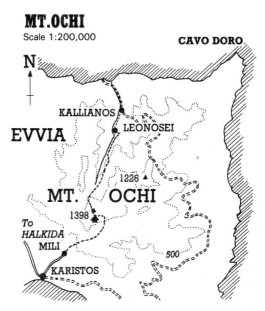

MT.OCHI

Scale 1:200,000

Mìli to Kallianòs

Walking time: 6½ hours

The path starts from the village of Mìli about 4km up the hill behind Kàristos. The simplest way to get to Mìli is by taxi. There is a bus, but the times are not likely to be convenient. The walk is pretty, up a winding lane between fields and olive groves, full of flowers in spring. There is a ruined Venetian castle and aqueduct off to the L. Mìli itself is surprisingly lush, its terraced gardens full of cherries, figs, walnuts and lioquats.

From the village café on, the road becomes a steep and bumpy track. Follow the road or the old mule path, which cuts off the corners, and in 10 minutes you come to the last house. On the L is a terrace with an ancient plane tree shading an abundant spring. Fill up with water; the next source is 3 hours away by the HAC refuge. You could sleep here, if necessary. There is a superb view over Kàristos and out to sea.

127

Mountain village

The path leads you back and forth across the stream until, after about 25 minutes, you come to a waterfall among large boulders at the foot of a cliff, where you cross to the R bank. 10 minutes later (35 mins) you cross back to the L for the last time. Past a clump of apple trees the path begins to veer away from the stream and climb ever more steeply up the R flank of the ravine through the trees. Man orchids, blue primulas, *orchis provincialis,* hellebores and *verbascum* are in abundance here.

At 1 hr you emerge from the woods into a grassy hollow far above the stream, close to the top of the ridge. Turn R across the hollow and a few moments later you come out on top of the ridge in a wide flowery meadow with a lone tall fir standing in the middle. Above you, at the top of a long steep slope you have an unimpeded view of the crags guarding the summit. An obvious gully runs down from just below the crags and passes to the R of the spur you are standing on. The trees reach to the edge of the gully. On the R the ground is bare for some distance.

128

The simplest route is straight up. Where your spur springs from the mountainside there is a wide gap in the trees, and above this point you can clearly see several paths winding down the slope. Strike up the slope. As long as you keep to the general direction, it does not matter which path you choose. About half-way up, cross to the R of the gully above a small waterfall, and then continue over rough grass to the foot of the crags (2 hrs). A little way below the crags is a spring where the stream that formed the gully rises.

From the spring a clear stony path leads uphill enclosed in a shallow gully. In 5 minutes you reach a fork. A good mule path branches L. On the R is a wall and an iron pole, all that is left of a sign indicating the refuge. Turn R. The wall is the end of a shed. The path passes behind it, on a level with the roof. From the roof you look down into a valley with fields and olive groves in the bottom. On the far side it rises to a rocky ridge.

The path bears L from the shed down into the valley bottom and becomes rather unclear. On the lower part of the opposite flank of the valley, diagonally across from the shed, there is a small cliff. Aim for the R edge of the cliff if you lose the path. Just below the corner of the cliff, on a slight rise, is a yellow sign forbidding shooting - visible from the shed. The path passes right by it.

In the valley bottom you cross one dry streambed (10 mins), quickly followed by another, overgrown by stunted planes. Turn briefly L up the bank of the second stream, with a fenced enclosure on your R, which you enter by a rough gate. Strike diagonally L uphill. In a few paces you are clear of the trees and can see the yellow sign ahead and slightly to your R. The path is non-existent here. Just aim for the sign (20 mins).

A clear path climbs the west flank of the valley, slanting R from the edge of the small cliff. In 15 minutes you come to a T-junction (35 mins). If you look L, you will see that you are almost on a level with several grey stone columns *(kolònes)* lying on the upper edge of the small cliff. The best thing is to head directly across to the columns. The path which leads up to the crags above is tiring and frustrating and keeps disappearing in the thorn bushes. It is easier going and more interesting to go via the columns and walk up the slabby rocks along the edge of the cliff.

These columns have lain where they are since these ancient quarry workings were abandoned. The grey stone is in fact cipollino marble and was much prized in Roman and Byzantine times. Several columns appear ready for shipment, colossal cylinders, smoothed and rounded, chiselled direct from the living rock. Heaven knows how they were moved. The quarrymen must have had a remarkably effective braking system to hold these monsters in check. A little way above the completed columns there are several only half-worked, not yet severed from the mother rock.

At the upper end of the cliff, beyond the quarry, you rejoin a clear well-trodden path (55 mins), which bears R towards the foot of the crags above. In 5 minutes (1 hr) you come to the edge of the bare rock. There, beneath a pointed conical rock, a well-paved *kalderéemee* climbs steeply up and over the rim of the ridge. Once on top of the ridge (1 hr 8 mins), you can see the sea again and the island of Andros off to the east. The ground underfoot is soft, reddish, gravelly soil.

The path descends gently L-ward into a gully. On your R the ground drops away to the sea. The slopes above and below the path are covered in heather (in flower in autumn) and low scrubby bushes. There are masses of autumn crocuses in October.

Over the gully, the path climbs back to the R and over a rounded spur, then in and out of another gully. At 1 hr 25 mins you pass through the rocks of a very prominent, jutting outcrop. A couple of minutes later, as the path bends back L over another rounded spur, you get your first glimpse of the rocky summit ridge. The actual summit is at the further end. You can also see Kastanólongos, the isolated chestnut wood that covers the slopes below the summit. Just ahead of you is a track. Ignore it and stay on the path, which bends back L into a gully which lower down develops into a sizeable ravine leading to the sea. Cross the gully (1 hr 35 mins), climb over another spur and again bend back L into a gully, where a skeletal lightning-struck tree stands by the path (1 hr 48 mins). On the ridge above are a few chestnut trees stunted by the salt wind. Round the next spur you come to the Kastanólongos wood (2 hrs), the greater part of which lies on the far side of the gully to your R.

Turn L up through the scattered trees along the L side of the gully until you emerge on to open ground by two or three substantial stone huts close to a stream. Cross the stream and climb the true L bank to the refuge, only a little further up (2 hrs 15 mins). At the L end of the refuge is the spring which feeds the stream. Behind it is the most southerly, tor-like peak in the summit ridge. The highest, Profítis Ilías, lies at the northern end. Fill up with water.

Face the front of the refuge, then cut across to your L until you join the clear stony path climbing the dry continuation of the gully into which the stream runs. In 20 minutes (2 hrs 35 mins), you reach a broad level saddle called Petrokándalo, between the southern end of the peak line on your R and a rounded height called Neräida off to the L. In front is a rocky outcrop sticking up out of the hillside, beyond which the ground slopes steeply down into a valley with fields and a track in the bottom. The far side is enclosed by a bare, rocky ridge. There is no clear path, but turn R and keep along the western edge of the now sheer crags of the summit ridge.

The valley on your L ends in a low grassy saddle slung between Òchi and the opposite wall of the valley. It forms the watershed between this valley and the Kallianòs ravine which declines north-east to the sea.

Keep along below the ridge until you reach a point beneath the last tor, where a tiny stream trickles from a spring. Climb up to the ridge ahead of you - your skyline (3 hrs). In front of you are some large outcrops overlooking the saddle mentioned above. From the edge of these rocks there is a sheer drop into a rocky amphitheatre, on whose further edge stands the forbidding-looking Judas *(yoòdhas)* peak.

To reach the Profítis Ilías peak, climb up the scree to the foot of the crag above you, then go up a couloir into the narrow gap between two rocky peaks. In the gap are the ruins of a sheepfold and right behind an almost perfectly preserved 6C BC temple dedicated to the goddess Hera (3 hrs 15 mins). It is made of big slabs of stone cut from the neighbouring rock. It is about 10 metres long by 2 metres high. A door leads into a single chamber. The only damage is to the roof, constructed of overlapping slabs, the middle row of which has caved in. I know of no other mountain-top temples. Profítis Ilías is the slabby peak opposite the temple. From the top you can see down the ravine to Kallianòs; it lies as far down as you can see though the houses are hidden by trees.

Go back down to the spring and on down to the grassy saddle. Towards the far end of the saddle, a well-trodden path descends (3 hrs 50 mins) into the Kallianòs ravine. Turn R, down the L bank of a stream. Cobbled in places, the path zigzags down L of the stream. At 3 hrs 58 mins you come to a plentiful spring at the foot of a group of knotty planes. 5 minutes further there is a second spring. Past a ruined hut, the path winds down towards the main stream in the bottom of the ravine. At 4 hrs 25 mins you cross this stream by a modern bridge. Thereafter the path follows the R bank through thick stands of plane and ilex. The stream tumbles and pours through a narrow, worn channel. The going is soft and earthy.

By 5 hrs 22 mins the ravine begins to open out a bit. There is a stretch of grass under the planes at the water's edge and a hut with a blue door on the far bank. On the R of the path is a stone shrine and just beyond it an enormous plane with a split trunk. A little further (5 hrs 25 mins) the ravine narrows to rocky jaws, where the stream tumbles down from pool to pool. The path descends by a regular stone staircase. The houses of Kallianós are visible ahead.

At 5 hrs 45 mins you pass a small well-kept church on the L with some plots of maize below. Beyond the church you cross a bridge over a tributary stream flowing down from the R and pass through the half-dozen cottages of Leonosèi *(leonosèyee),* surrounded by pomegranate and judas trees, lemon and orange, olive and cypress, and tiny fields of maize and sprouts. The path continues along above the houses.

At 6 hrs 2 mins you cross a stream on the far side of the village, where the path bears L and begins to climb. In 20 minutes you reach the first houses of Kallianós. A further 5 minutes takes you to the church of Áyii Taxiárches *(àyee taxeeyàrhes)* (6 hrs 25 mins), where the dirt road back to Káristos begins.

Getting back is a matter of patiently waiting for bus or truck. And there is always the beach half an hour or so further, at the very end of the ravine.

XEROVOUNI (1417m)

Map: NSSG 1:200,000 sheet Evvias

Though lower than Mt Dírfi, Xerovoúni *(kserovoònee)* is craggier and more precipitous and the walk up is much more interesting, through a beautiful wooded ravine from the village of Kambià *(kambyà),* full of flowers and unspoilt even by a forest track. Access is the same as for Dírfi. As you come out of Káto Stení, take a R turn signposted Kambia 2km.

Kambià to Xerovoúni

Walking time: 3 hours

The general direction of your route is absolutely clear. Stand in Kambià looking up the ravine behind the village. You can see the cliffs which guard the summit at the head of the ravine. The point you are aiming for is the L (north-west) corner of the cliffs, where they rise from the long Mesórahi ridge. The route lies up the ravine, up to the R on to the spur that forms the R flank of the ravine, then straight up to the cliffs.

Go through Kambià, continuing straight ahead from the end of the road. A good path leads up the true R bank of a stream in the shade of plane trees. On your L is a steep slope covered with low scrub and herbs, where there is a profusion of flowers in May: cistus, broom, yellow Jerusalem sage, colonies of yellow orchids. The slopes to your R are much steeper and covered with Greek Fir, whose light-green new growth is surprisingly soft and velvety compared with the harsh prickliness of the old needles.

From the corner of the cliffs above the spring there appears to be a good steep scrambling route to the summit; I have only been part of the way up.

The normal route is as follows. To the L of this corner, as you face it with your back to Dírfi, a path climbs obliquely L to a point on your immediate skyline where there is a jutting tooth-like rock. When you reach this point you are on the edge of a wide bowl of grey scree enclosed by cliffs. The path continues into the bowl in the same direction as before; there are paint splodges to mark the way. Above you to the R, at the apex of a roughly triangular run of scree, is a steep couloir, the only obvious way up between two walls of rock. Cross the scree in front of you, L-ward and upward, as far as the rock wall ahead. Turn R along the wall to the start of the couloir (3 hrs). It is about 5 minutes' scramble to the top of the couloir, where, turning L, you see the summit - a rocky bump - right in front of you: a matter of moments.

Descent by the same route takes about two hours. Alternatively, you can walk the length of the Mesórahi ridge to meet the Steni-Stróbones track below Dírfi.

MT.ATHOS

Scale 1:200,000

N

To LERISSOS

OURANOPOLIS

ESFIGMENOU
HILANDARI
ZOGRAFOU
VATOPEDI
KONSTAMONITOU
DOCHIARIOU
XENOFONTOS
ROSSIKO
PANTOKRATOROS
STAVRONIKITA
KARYES
KOUTLOUMOUSSIOU
IVIRON
XEROPOTAMOU
DAFNI
SIMOPETRA
GRIGORIOU
DIONYSIOU
AYIOU PAVLOU
AYIA ANNAO
KARAKALLOU
FILOTHEOU
MT. ATHOS
2033
KERASIA
LAVRA
PRODROMOU

1042

200
510
500

NORTHERN GREECE

MT.ATHOS (2033m)
Map: NSSG 1:200,000 sheet Halkidikis

Mt Athos, the monks' republic, must be one of the most beautiful and fascinating places on earth, both for its scenery and its monasteries, with their amazing architecture, art treasures and medieval monastic life. It is mostly virgin forest, having never been cultivated or grazed. The flowers in consequence are glorious, both in number and variety. To make the most of a visit, take a guide book and, if possible, read something like Sydney Loch's *Athos: The Holy Mountain* before you go. I would strongly recommend Easter for a visit; you get the rituals of the church, the flowers, snow on the mountain and good weather all together. But you won't get any food: there is strict fasting through Holy Week!

Getting to Athos is a bit of a hassle. You need a letter of recommendation from your consulate in Athens (Ploutárchou 1, Kolonàki - for the British), or Thessaloniki (Vas. Konstantìnou 39) -just a formality. Present the letter, in Athens, at the Ministry of Foreign Affairs (Zalakòsta 2: Mon-Fri 1100-1300), in Thessaloniki, at the Ministry for Northern Greece (Platèia Diikitirìou, Rm 218). They issue permits for 4 days only and you have to use it within a month. Present the permit at the Aliens Police in Thessaloniki (Polytechnìou 41), who will fix the first day of your visit.

There are buses from Thessaloniki (terminus at Karakàsi 68) to Ouranòpolis, whence one boat a day leaves for Dàfni *(dhàfnee)*, the port of Athos, at 10 a.m. To catch the boat you need to get the 6 a.m. bus. But Ouranòpolis is no bad place to stay; there are some fine beaches. Stock up with food. Monastic fare is frugal, even when there is not a fast on. You cannot brew up in the monasteries, but you will be thankful for something on the march.

Women, unfortunately, are not allowed beyond Ouranòpolis.

The boat journey lasts two hours. You surrender your passport and permit as you board. On arrival at Dàfni, take the bone-shaker bus to Karyès, the administrative centre. There, go first to the police to recover your passport, then to the yellow building in the main square - the seat of the ruling body - to receive your 'diamonitirion' *(dheeyamoneeteèreeyo)*, the document which entitles you to free board and lodging at any monastery. Remember: monastery gates shut at sunset.

I recommend a clockwise trip round the peninsula, down the east coast and back up the west. By the time the permit-granting formalities are over, it will be late afternoon. As soon as you can, head for the monasteries of Stavronikíta or Ivìron for the first night. Ivìron shortens the next day's journey by an hour. Stavronikíta is smaller, but more dramatic, architecturally and in terms of its communal life. Stick to the track, to be safe. Go past Koutloumoussíou monastery right next to Karyès and keep L at the first fork. Stavronikíta is about an hour to the L down a branch track, as you get down towards the sea. Walking time to either monastery is 2-3 hours by the track.

Note: Walking times on the east coast of Athos are very rough estimates. I had not conceived the idea of making a book when I visited!

Stavronikíta to Ivìron

Walking time: 1 hour.

The path circles the garden fence and leads down to the sea. Keep along the shore until (30 mins) you reach the beach by a fortified tower. Turn up R on to the track and continue L down to Ivìron.

Caiques ply the coast from Ierissos at the northern end of the Athos peninsula to Ivìron, and on down to Ayìa Làvra *(aeèya làvra)*, the oldest (96 AD) and largest of the monasteries, at the eastern foot of Mt.Athos itself. If you are footsore or short of time, you can always do a stretch by sea.

Ivìron to Ayìa Làvra

Walking time: 6-7 hours.

Go along the shore past the meadow in front of Ivìron. Cross the bridge over the stream at the end of the wall and go up the lane opposite, past a pretty blue-washed chapel on the L. From here to the tower of Karakàllou *(karakàloo)* - about 2 hours - the track rises and falls over headlands and spurs, keeping always a short distance inland. The going is soft and comfortable. You pass the outlying dependencies of various monasteries. Here and there a stream crosses the track. At the only fork, the R branch leads uphill to the monastery of Filothèou. Keep L down to the sea and the tower (about 2 hours).

(If you don't want to do the whole journey from Stavronikíta to Làvra in one day, you can stop off at Filothèou or Karakàllou - both a little way inland.)

Beyond the tower, the path climbs steadily inland. As you go higher, the scrub gives way to evergreen oak and sweet chestnut. The woods are glorious. Out of the woods at last you begin a long, winding descent to the sea again at the bay of Morfonoú, below the ruined tower of the Amalfitans, which stands on a wooded hilltop with the crags of Athos, the Holy Mountain itself, rising in the background. The path zigzags down to a tree-filled ravine, where a river runs out to the sea. Over a concrete bridge and along the edge of the beach to the end by a sawmill belonging to the monastery of Filothéou (3-3½ hours). There is a fountain at the end, and a muddy path leads uphill on to a track. Turn L.

Keep a sharp lookout for the continuation of the path. On the L, on the outside of a slight R-hand bend, not very far up the track, it goes down into the woods again. There are cobbles underfoot, then proper steps, and the telephone line goes that way - a sure route-marker. Past a ruined cottage on the R, the path burrows clear and soft into the depths of the wood. Springs and streams abound. You cross several mossy, ancient bridges. Beyond the woods, eventually, giant tree-heather has grown over the path and it is a wearisome task pushing your way through. You go in and out of endless gullies, straining to see the way ahead and locate the next telephone pole. The sea is far below to the L, the mountain way ahead, and you begin to wonder whether your sufferings will ever end!

About 2 hours from Morfonoú (say, 5½ hours altogether), the path touches the shore. You cross an old high-backed bridge. There is about an hour to go. As you top each rise and get a view ahead, you can see dark points of cypress trees on a spur at the foot of the eastern ridge of the mountain. They mark the site of Ayía Lávra.

Eventually, your tunnel of heather and scrub disgorges you on to a track, where you turn L and come, in a few minutes, to the monastery gate.

Enclosed within its ancient walls, Ayía Lávra is like a small town. See the blood red church, the original refectory and its frescoes, and the treasury, full of ancient manuscripts and gifts from Byzantine emperors.

Ascent of Mt.Athos

Walking time: 3-4 hours

From Kerasiá climb back on to the main path and continue L until you come to the saddle between Mt.Carmel and the rising ridge

Mountain monastery

behind Kerasià. There is a bronze signpost at the foot of a gnarled oak, pointing the way (R) to Athos. A few metres up the path there is a clearing with a water trough. (Hide the bulk of your gear in the undergrowth: you have to come back this way). The path continues up a well-worn channel through prickly scrub, before climbing steeply up an exposed spur. You look down on the roofs of Àyia

Ánna and the monastery of Grigoríou *(greegoréeyoo)* on the shore a little further north.

At the top of the spur the path levels out and enters a small oak wood. Keep R at the junction in the middle of the wood. Bearing R you come out in the open again above the ridge overlooking Kerasiá. The path bends L, following the contour, along the L side of a gully through a very open oak wood. Cross to the R of the gully into fir trees, out into sparse oak, then back to the L of the gully. The trees are getting thinner. Above on the L is a long grey slope rising to the skyline.

Ayìa Làvra to Kerasiá

Walking time: 3 hours

Kerasiá *(kerasyà)* - Cherry tree - is a good base for climbing Mt.Athos itself. It is a *skiti*, not a monastery; that is, a sort of rural cell, dependent on a monastery, inhabited by monks who have chosen to live a more reclusive life.

Turn L out of Làvra gate - Kerasiá is signposted - along a good *kalderèemee* leading uphill under the spurs of the mountain. Keep R and up. After about an hour you reach a point more or less directly above the Roumanian monastery of Prodròmou, where, by a chapel and the wooden cross of Koukouzélis, the path bends abruptly R, with fine views north and south. Round this corner, the path continues on the level as far as a fork, where what appears to be the main path bears downhill to the L. The uphill branch, which is nonetheless the right way, looks most uncertain for the first few paces, but soon improves.

The scrub begins to give way to small trees, mostly oak. Past a wild olive tree with a water pipe and tap wired to its branches, the gradient increases and you enter the woods again, pine at first, then firs, chestnut and oak. There are numerous springs. In an hour or so (2-2½ hours) you come to a neat signpost indicating Kerasia down to the L and Àyia Ànna *(àeeyàna)* straight on. Go L. You lose height rapidly and come to another fork by a spring and water trough - the beginning of Kerasiá. Down to the R is a gaudy church with a green dome. A couple of terraces below it, a severe stone house is the headquarters of the *skiti*. The monks will put you up and feed you frugally, but be as polite and discreet as possible.

The site of Kerasiá is spectacular, about 1000 metres above the sea, enclosed between two arms of mountain. The western one is Mt.Carmel.

The old mule road

The path tends R-ward with a small rounded height above the gully to your R. Before long a grey squat building comes in sight on a level platform of ground directly in front of you - the chapel of the Panayìa *(panaeèya)* or Virgin Mary (about 2 hours from the signpost). You could camp here. There is a well inside the chapel - bucket provided.

Above the chapel, a wide shallow gully leads to a ridge, rising R-ward to an apex of white-grey rock. Head up the gully to the ridge, then scramble up R to the summit (about 3 hours). There is a tremendous drop on the far side, and views all up the peninsula. They say you can see Istanbul on a clear, day, but perhaps that is wishful thinking. You can certainly see Mt.Olympus across the sea to the south-west. Right on the summit is the chapel of the Transfiguration, with a great iron cross dated 1897 beside it.

Kerasià to Àyia Ànna

Walking time: 1½-2 hours

From the start of the Athos ascent path, keep straight on. You descend gently through the woods until, abruptly, you find yourself at the brink of the huge limestone cliffs that beetle over Àyia Ànna. There follows a ferocious descent of some 800 metres over loose stones - luckily, in the shade.

Àyia Ànna is a very pretty 'village' of whitewashed monkish cells scattered over the steep hillside above the sea. Hung with vines and wistaria, the houses stand among ancient terraces of rich, black soil. There is water everywhere. The path brings you out by the church, where the guest quarters are also located.

Àyia Ànna to Dàfni

Walking time: 5½ hours

Turn R at the church in Àyia Ànna and you come to the monastery of Ayìou Pàvlou *(aèeyoo pàvloo)* after an easy three quarters of an hour. Turn down to the sea and along a track behind the beach until you come to the foot of a cliff, where there appears to be no way forward. Go down on to the beach, round a jutting cliff, over a plank bridge and there, in front of you, the path continues straight up the cliffside. You reach the monastery of Dionysìou *(dheeyonee-seèyoo),* one of the most picturesque, in 30 minutes (1 hr 15 mins). Continue along the shore for a bit, up another steep ascent and down into a verdant little gully with a bridge over a stream. After 1½ hours (2 hrs 45 mins) you reach Grigorìou *(greegoreèyoo).* A little way beyond there is a fork, where a good *kaldereemee* continues uphill to the R and a path marked 'Sìmonos Pètras *(dàsos)'* branches L. Go L down to the sea where there is a shingle beach. Then begins a long disheartening climb to the monastery of Sìmonos Pètras or Simôpetra, perched on a pinnacle of rock some 300 metres up (3 hrs 30 mins). Dàfni is another 2 hours (5 hrs 30 mins) along a sandy track - keep downhill to the L at the only junction. It is possible to continue up the coast to the Russian monastery and beyond.

GAMÌLA (2497m)

Map: NSSG 1:200,000 sheet Ioanninon

Gamìla *(gameéla)*, or Tìmfi as it is called on the map, is an excellent mountain for the walker. Though the southern and central parts are rather bare, there are dramatic rock formations, two stupendous 1000-metre gorges, a couple of long traverse routes, transhumant shepherds, notable flora, and some very pretty villages. It is also easy to link up with the neighbouring Mt.Smolikas, which is much greener and wetter. You could easily fill a week to ten days of leisurely walking in the area, and you eat and lodge slightly better than par for the mountains! If you don't feel like too much uphill work in the heat, the gentle gradients of the dirt roads that circle the southern flanks of both mountains are a beautiful substitute. (For Mt.Smolikas and other Gamìla routes, see Part Two, pages 96, and 91.)

Access is easiest from Yànnina. There are buses to Pàpingo, Monodèndri and the other Zagòri villages on the south side of Gamìla, though not every day. It is hitchable - with patience. There are, however, daily buses to Kònitsa *(kòneetsa)*, which stop at Kleidonià *(kleedhonyà)*, a village near the Voidomàtis *(voydhomàt-ees)* river bridge about 12 km south of Konitsa. There is a path from there to Pàpingo *(pàpeengo)* in 3 hours.

Kleidonià to Pàpingo

Walking time: 3 hours

Stand at the *magazèe* where the bus stops, facing the steep ridge dominating the village to the east. On the other side of the road a lane leads to the foot of the ridge. Follow the lane round to the R. Turn off L up a path over open ground to the chapel you can see from the *magazèe*. From there on, the path is clear all the way to the ridge.

Just over the top there is a chapel on the L and the original, now nearly deserted village of Kleidonià, a couple of hundred metres further on. You can see the mouth of the Vìkos gorge *(vèekos)* some way to the east.

Go through the village (1 hr). Beyond is a gully, the further slope rising to a low ridge with a clump of trees on the top. Go up to the trees and turn L along the top of the ridge until you come to a solitary tree. That was the advice given me by an old man. Impatiently, I took the advice of a younger man who said there was a

142

shortcut.

I turned L in the gully, then R when I came to a fork. As I could not see a path I climbed out on the R, got entangled in the scrub, and was forced back into the gully, where I found a path on the L which leads to the solitary tree where the main path comes down from the ridge. It would probably have been better to take the main path in the first place.

At the lone tree the path turns R and descends gently to what appears to be a junction. Keep L and up over a rise, then down a broad stony stretch into a gully with abandoned fields on the far side. Cross the gully and turn sharp R. The path follows the contour in and out of numerous re-entrants. You get the impression you are moving far too far over to the L, until you come to a more substantial gully with sides of stepped and slabby rock. Cross it, and the path begins to work back towards the R. The towers of Astràka, the peak that hangs over Pàpingo, loom ahead of you. You reach Pàpingo about 2 hours after leaving old Kleidhonià (3 hrs).

It is a well-preserved and pretty village, built in the characteristic style of the Zagòri: solid stone houses enclosed by semi-fortified walls and porches, with their living quarters upstairs. The original living-rooms were *ontàdhes*, in the Turkish style, that is, bordered with raised platforms strewn with rugs and cushions for reclining. The roofs are tiled in great slabs of schist. Traditionally, there was a lot of woodwork, carved ceilings, panelling and so on, but not much survives.

Pàpingo is more accustomed to foreign visitors, including walkers, than most other places. The *magazèe*, whose proprietor also holds the key to the Gamìla refuge *(katafèeyo),* is relatively sophisticated and accustomed to serving proper meals. There is a guesthouse nearby. The river bottom below Pàpingo, though a long way down, makes a great place for camping.

The refuge, which is 3 hours' climb from the upper village of Pàpingo, known as *meekrò pàpeengo* or *pàno mahalà,* can be seen from the terrace of the *magazèe.* It lies on the very obvious col between the towers of Astràka on the R and the rounded peak of Làpatos on the L. The snag about using the refuge, apart from the expense, is that you have to come back to Pàpingo to return the key.

Pàpingo to Kepèsovo via refuge

Walking time: 8 hours

To get to the upper village, go down the lane from the *magazèe* to the church, turn L and out on the road. It is about 30 minutes' walk up the road.

The track ends in the *platèeya* by the church. A cobbled lane leads L out of the top L corner. At the end of it a sign points to the refuge giving the time of ascent as 3 hours. The path soon turns back to the R and begins to loop steadily uphill through patches of rough pasture and thickets of oak and hazel. Past the Antàlki *(andàlkee)* spring you climb an exhausting slope of steep loose soil and stone. As you gain height the oak and hazel give way to scattered firs.

About an hour above Antàlki you come to the Tràfos spring. 20 minutes above Tràfos is a R fork for the ascent of Astràka (2436m), about 2 hours; the world's second deepest straight-down pothole starts on the ridge, 415 metres in one long drop - known locally as the *provateèna* cave. 15 minutes above the fork is the Kròuna spring and 20 minutes beyond that, the refuge - bestriding the narrow saddle below the Astràka peak (3 hrs).

The ground drops away abruptly on the north side of the refuge into a valley with two small tarns, known as *stànee tsoomànee* after the Sarakatsan family that has traditionally made its summer *stànee* or sheepfold there. Across the valley opposite the refuge is the Plòskos peak and to the R the Gamìla or Avàlos peak itself, reached in about 3 hours. To the L of Plòskos on the lip of the Aòòs ravine overlooking Kònitsa is the small lake of Drakòlimni *(dhrakòleem-nee)*.

If you are going to camp, do so by the refuge, not in the *stànee tsoomànee* valley because of the sheepdogs - to say nothing of the beautiful sunset view of the mountains of Albania.

For Kepèsovo, descend to the smaller of the two tarns and round the R-hand end to where a gully comes in beneath the north face of Astràka. Go up the grassy slope on the far side of the gully and head south-east parallel to the Astràka cliffs, keeping them 200-300 metres to your R. Keep L of the gully at the foot of the cliffs and R of the next one over. It is easy going over grassy pastures at first, then up and down over bare rounded hillocks. Aim for a rounded hillock some way ahead with a cairn on top - visible from the refuge.

After about 1 hour (4 hrs) you reach a small tarn at the foot of the knoll with the cairn. Leaving the tarn on your L, proceed to the point below the cairn where the gound drops away and you get a view of the way ahead.

The ground falls away into a gentle grassy valley with a shepherd's hut. On the R, it is enclosed by a spur running out from Astraka; on the L, by rocky slopes rising towards the jagged eastern peak line. Dead ahead, cutting right across your line of march, is the Mègas Làkos ravine which runs into the Víkos gorge over to your R.

Go down past the shepherd's hut. A well-worn path keeps to the R side of the deepening gully on your L. About 50 minutes (4 hrs 50 mins) from the cairn, at the foot of a large rocky bastion, the path begins to zigzag down L into the bottom of the Mègas Làkos ravine. It crosses over and climbs back to a comparable height on the far side, following the flank of the ravine now at the foot of a huge wall of dripping rock. Ahead the ravine bends R towards the hazy depths of Víkos. Close to the path there is a low cave-like opening where a spring of icy water wells up into a little pool. A short distance beyond it, there is a narrow opening in the L wall of the ravine. Turn up L into this breach on a path that keeps to the R of the dry gully running down its middle. The path turns R up and over the rim of the ravine on to the flat top of a ridge, past a muddy pool in a hollow, then out on to the eastern edge of the ridge overlooking the Tsepèlovo-Skamnèli road and the endless wooded ridges receding into the distance towards Mètsovo.

Keep L at a fork - the R branch appears to lead back to the Mègas Làkos. The path climbs a little and passes over a series of rounded grassy bumps. From being earthy and dusty, it changes to gritty and shaly. You begin to descend towards the village of Vradèto *(vradhèto)*, not in sight. A track is visible ahead. The path goes down between two patches of pillar-like rock formations, keeping closer to the R towards a gully. The slopes here are open and treeless, the gradient gentle.

Down over this largely featureless slope, leaving a rocky patch to your L and the gully to your R, you pass R-handed round a small hummock and on to the track. R leads to Vradèto and L to Kepèsovo, a distance of 4 or 5 kilometres. A little way along to the L (opposite a flat grassy platform on the R) and about 150 metres L of the track is another of the straight-down Gamìla pot-holes , *ee trèepa tees nèefees* - The Bride's Hole!

Víkos Gorge: Pàpingo to Monodèndri

Walking time: 7-8 hours

With Samaria in Crete this is the best gorge walk in Greece. It is hard

145

work up or down, and the amount of time it takes depends on how easily you find the path. There are places where it is easily lost, though you won't get lost. You can't. The 1000-metre walls of the gorge funnel you through to Monodéndri willy-nilly, but you can cause yourself a lot of extra hardship.

Between Pàpingo and the Astràka cliffs which overlook it runs a steep narrow valley. The path to the mouth of the Vìkos gorge runs along the further side of it at approximately the same altitude as Pàpingo. The easiest place to get on it is at Mikrò Pàpingo where it starts. It is, however, possible to join it from Pàpingo main village.

Start up the track to Mìkro Pàpingo. It bends sharply L into a re-entrant past a spring. Just beyond the angle of the re-entrant an overgrown track turns down to the R to the banks of a stream. Go down the R bank of the stream until the track turns to cross it. Continue up the slope opposite until eventually you meet the path coming along the valleyside from Mikrò Pàpingo. The junction is pretty much on a level with Mikrò Pàpingo. In fact, you can see some of the village houses back to your L. Turn R. The path follows the contour, at first, through scattered trees and the remains of fields before gaining height a little over scrubby, rocky ground, until, beneath a markedly red patch on the cliffs overhead, it begins to descend and bear away to the L.

You come to a fork where both L and R branches descend almost equally steeply. Take the L branch, which leads almost at once to two broad runs of scree beneath sheer cliffs. Cross the first scree, where there is a fearsome view upwards to the foot of the giant pinnacles of rock that stand sentinel over this corner of the gorge. There is a bare thread of path to the second scree. Cross that too. Thereafter, the path is little more than a goat trail. Pass a signpost pointing back to Mikrò and Megàlo Pàpingo. Pass above a group of strangely weathered rocks that stick up like eroded teeth from the steep slope. The path turns L into the beginnings of the gorge and winds down a dry slope. It quickly loses definition, but if you keep going diagonally downhill at a fairly steep angle you come out on the banks of the Voidomàtis river by some indeterminate ruins.

I hesitate to give a time for this stage of the walk, for I spent the best part of three hours finding the way. Perhaps two hours or a little more would be nearer the mark (2 hrs 30 mins). The bed of the gorge is quite dry between June and September, and the river literally boils out of the rocks at this end.

Cross to the true L bank of the river and turn L upstream. An easy path follows the edge of a strip of meadow along the river bank. The gorge narrows as you go, both sides rising sheer for several hundred metres. Gradually the bottom of the gorge fills with trees: a welcome relief from the heat of the sun, which seems to be trapped and concentrated between the cliffs.

After an hour and ten minutes (3 hrs 40 mins), you come to a small white shrine and a spring softly filling a dark pool beneath a rock, where there is a cup for the thirsty passer-by. The path continues along the same (L) bank to where the Mègas Làkos ravine comes in from the L (4 hrs 40 mins). The path temporarily fades here in a patch of scree. Climb diagonally up the scree until you hit a clear path again - you can see it from below: not far. Continue along it for 20 minutes (5 hrs) until you descend to the river again by a boulder marked with a red arrow. 50 metres upstream on the opposite bank is a stream gully by a boulder marked with a small cairn. Scramble up the lip of the gully and you will find the path again on the R. (It is possible to make your way up the riverbed, but it is extremely tiring clambering over, and under, the house-sized boulders.) Continue up the R bank for about 20 minutes (5 hrs 20 mins) - the path is scarcely more than a *sèerma* (literally, a 'wire', i.e. a bare thread) through the trees; then clamber up L round a large rock blocking the direct way ahead. 10 minutes later (5 hrs 30 mins) you descend to the riverbed. The gorge opens out a bit here. 20 minutes further upstream (5 hrs 50 mins) you come to a cairn with a stick pointer on a rock in the riverbed. Monodèndri *(monodhèndree)* is above you at this point, high on the southern rim of the gorge, on your R. Though you cannot see the houses, the 14C monastery of Àyia Paraskevì is visible on the edge of a crag. On your L, another trench-like ravine leads back towards the village of Vradèto. The path up to Monodèndri starts in the trees on your R. Steep and slippery at first, it turns into a paved walkway at the top and enters the village along the side of the church. In fact, it takes you right into the plane-shaded *platèeya* (6 hrs 30 mins), by the principal *magazèe*.

Beyond the *magazèe,* a lane leads to the Àyia Paraskevì monastery mentioned above, where a tiny path continues on round the sheer cliffside to the inaccessible bolt-hole the villagers used to use in times of danger.

Though it is the finest, and most touristy - though that does not amount to much as yet - of the Zagòri villages, Monodèndri has no rentable accommodation, but no one seems to mind if you sleep on

147

the ground by the church. The nearest hotel - very attractive in a restored traditional house - is at Vìtsa, a 15 minute walk away.

OLYMPUS (2917m)

Map: NSSG 1:200,000 sheet Larisis

At 2917 metres Mt Olympus *(òleembos)* is the highest mountain in Greece. Rising more or less straight out of the sea on the western shore of the Thermaic Gulf it is also the most dramatic and beautiful. It is covered in dense forest of beech, Black and Balkan Pine. Its wild flower population is without parallel even in Greece, and includes several rare endemics, among them the lovely blue *jankaea heldreichii*. The greater part of the massif is now a national park, and picking any of the flowers is stricly out of order.

The village of Litòhoro *(leetòhoro)* at the eastern foot of the massif is the best base for walkers. It is 405 km by road from Athens and 90 km from Thessalonìki. It is also accessible by rail, on the main Athens-Thessalonìki line, though the station is 9 km from the village. There are buses from Katerìni and Thessalonìki.

Litòhoro has several hotels and a Youth Hostel, as well as several camp sites by the sea 4 or 5 km away. The nicest and nearest of these is the Olympus Beach, with a fine sandy beach and a very attractive plane-shaded outdoor taverna called Plàka right next door.

The HAC has an information kiosk in the main square in Litòhoro, where you can get a booklet showing the main routes and refuges on the mountain.

There are two main refuges on the east side of Olympus. The Spìlios Agapitòs (refuge A), at 2100 metres, is run by Kòstas Zolòtas, a native of Litòhoro, who has a German wife. They both speak good English. The refuge sleeps 90 and is manned from May to about October 15th. It gets pretty crowded, with foreigners mainly, in August, so it might be wise to book a place (refuge telephone number: 0352.81.800).

The Yosos Apostolidis hut (belonging to the Thessaloniki club, SEO) is on the so-called Plateau of the Muses *(pedheeyàdha ton moosòn)* at 2700 metres. It is manned in July and August only, though there is an enclosed porch you can shelter in at other times. It is more primitive than refuge A and much less frequented. Its situation is spectacular.

148

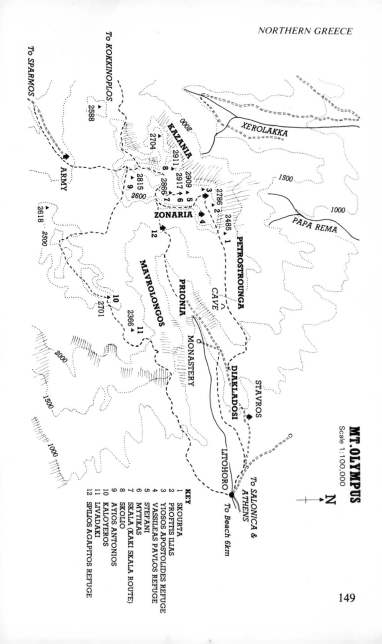

MT. OLYMPUS

Scale 1:100,000

N

To SALONICA &
ATHENS

To Beach 6km

KEY
1 SKOURTA
2 PROFITIS ILIAS
3 YIOSOS APOSTOLIDES REFUGE
4 VASSILEAS PAVLOS REFUGE
5 STEFANI
6 MYTIKAS
7 SKALA (KAKI SKALA ROUTE)
8 SKOLIO
9 AYIOS ANTONIOS
10 KALOYEROS
11 LIVADAKI
12 SPILIOS AGAPITOS REFUGE

149

There is a third refuge on the Plateau of the Muses, the King Paul *(vasseelèyas pàvlos)*, but for that you have to get the keys from Zolòtas.

No special expertise is needed to climb Olympus in favourable conditions (winter climbs are another matter). The mountain, however, is notoriously fickle - something to do with being so close to the sea. Even on a hot summer day the weather can take a sudden and nasty turn, with lightning, snow and hail suceeding each other in a space of minutes. Patches of frozen snow block the path, especially in the Zonària area, until mid-June. I personally have witnessed a near-fatal accident because of that. In other words, treat Olympus with respect.

To reach the start of the walking routes you have to take the forest track, which winds 18km up the north flank of the Enipèas ravine to Priònia *(preeyònya)*. Without a car, you will probably have to take a taxi, except in high season, when there is a good chance of a lift.

At kilometre 14, the spot known as Diaklàdosi *(dheeyaklàdhosee)*, there are two large signs on the R of the track displaying maps of the paths. One of them begins right here, leading up R to the Yòsos Apostolídis hut in 6 hours of hard work!

Priònia to the summit, Mỳtikas

Walking time: 5 hours

1km short of Priònia a track leads into the bottom of the ravine, to the ruined monastery of Àyios Dionỳsios, destroyed by the Germans in 1943 on suspicion of harbouring Resistance fighters.

Priònia is a beautiful spot, surrounded by greenery and dominated by towering crags. There is a small taverna-cum-snack bar, which provides a basic meal. Do not be surprised to find a lot of people about in summer. Fill up with water; there is no more until refuge A.

The path begins just uphill from the taverna. An HAC signpost indicates the way, giving the time to the refuge as 2½ hours. Cross a stream with a small waterfall on your R and start to climb steeply up through woods of beech and Black Pine. The path is well-trodden and there is no danger of losing the way. As you gain height there are superb views across the Mavrolongos ravine to your L and up to the summits above your head.

Refuge A perches on the edge of an abrupt spur surrounded by huge, storm-beaten specimens of Balkan Pine. Zolotas, the warden,

Mt. Olympus - looking into the Cauldron. Photo: Alistair Scott

runs a tight ship, so get into his good books as you enter by exchanging your boots for a pair of the slippers provided, and make yourself known to him. Let him know in good time if you want a meal and bed or are just passing through. I strongly recommend staying the night to enjoy the food, log fire, company and glorious sunset and dawn views. If the price seems steep, just remember that everything has to be brought up by mule.

Zolotas knows Olympus like the back of his hand and has done many of the rock-climbing routes himself. If approached courteously, he will give any advice you want.

It is best to make an early start for the summit - best of all, if you can start before dawn to be on the summit at dawn. Cloud often gathers on the peaks in the middle of the day, and that sometimes means a storm in the afternoon or early evening - not a pleasant experience if you are caught in an exposed place.

Fill up with water. The next source is at the Yosos Apostolidis hut, when it is open.

The path continues behind the refuge, climbing L-handed up a steep spur among the last of the trees. After an hour (3 hrs 30 mins) you come to a signpost.

151

There are two possible routes to Mýtikas, one via the ridge known as *kakeè skàla,* the other via the Loùki *(loôkee)* couloir. The first goes more or less straight ahead up the R flank of the featureless stony valley in front of you, with the peak of Ayios Antonios on the L. You reach the summit ridge after about an hour (4 hrs 30 mins) between the peaks of Skolio *(skolyò)* on the L and Skàla on the R. You know when you have arrived because there is a 500-metre sheer drop on the other side, into the chasm of Kazania - the Cauldrons.

The *kakeè skàla* - Rotten Stairway - begins in a narrow cleft on the R just short of the ridge. Paint splashes mark the way. It is a modest scramble in dry weather. The route keeps just below the ridge, so you are protected from the drop into Kazania. The drop on your R is steep, but not sheer. It can be alarming for someone unused to heights, but there is no real danger. No bad thing to have a length of rope for the nervous or children.

The route starts with a slightly descending R-ward traverse to a narrow nick in the ridge line revealing the drop to Kazania - it is easily negotiated. Continue traversing R, skirting the base of the Skala peak, then climb L up a steepish gully made a little awkward by loose rock on sloping footholds. Bear R at the top over steep, but reassuringly solid rock, and through a narrow neck. Step L round an awkward corner and there, in front of you, scarcely 100 metres away, is Mýtikas, a narrow boulder-strewn platform with a trig point, tin Greek flag and summit book. It takes about 40 minutes from the beginning of *kakeè skàla* (5¼ hours *in toto).*

On a clear day you can see Mt Smòlikas and all the peaks of the Pindos range to the west, Parnassòs in the south, Mt Athos in the north-east.

Just north of Mýtikas is the Stefàni peak (2909m), known also as the Throne of Zeus. It is a bristling, precipitous hog's back closing off the north side of the Kazània cirque. As you can see from Mýtikas, there are a couple of nastily exposed moves to scale the last few feet.

The second route leads R at the signpost, above refuge A, up and over the rounded spur above you, then all along the tilting striations of rock known as Zonària *(zonàreeya),* that lie directly beneath the tooth-like pinnacles which guard the summit area. The path here is cut by several gullies, which hold deep wedges of snow until mid-to-late June. Crossing them requires care without an ice axe.

After about 40 minutes, just before the highest point in the path, a

Mt. Olympus -Kaki Skala. Photo: Alistair Scott

signpost indicates the Yosos Apostolidis (SEO) hut in 20 minutes.
The start of the Loùki couloir is just up to the L, leading to Mỳtikas
in about 45 minutes (5 hours *in toto* by this route). It is a steep, but
easy scramble. A couple of moves at the top are airy, but not
dangerous. I like this route, although Zolòtas strongly counsels
against it, for it is exposed to rock-falls when there are other people
on it. Descending this way saves a good two hours if you are going on
to the SEO hut.

Mỳtikas to SEO hut

Walking time: 2½ hours via Kakì Skàla, 1 hour via Loùki

In either case you have to make your way back to the signpost on the
Zonària path below Loùki. If you ascend Mỳtikas via Kakì Skàla and
want to come down Loùki, the mouth of the couloir is just a few
metres north of the summit and, though it may appear that any move
in that direction will lead to instant immortality, you are in fact quite
safe.

Beyond the signpost you turn downhill to the L below the north-
east face of Stefàni. The Plateau of the Muses is on your R across an
intervening corrie, bounded to the west by the Toùmba and Profìtis
Ilìas peaks, with the Yòsos Apostolidis (SEO) hut between them (5½

153

hours). (This section of path is very exposed to avalanching in winter.) Toúmba and Profítis Ilías can be climbed in 20 minutes or so; the chief interest is the view. A small herd of chamois *(agreeyokàtseeka)* still survives on Olympus and can often be seen in this area, especially towards evening.

SEO hut to Diakladosi

Walking time: 4½ hours

This is a beautiful, but long and tiring descent, which brings you out on the forest track to Priónia (see above).

With your back to the refuge, turn L and continue to the edge of the Plateau of the Muses, where the path bends R round the head of a precipitous drop. Thence it follows the ridge dividing the Enipéas ravine on your R from the Pàpa Rèma ravine to the north as far as a rounded bump with a survey point on top. Here, the coarse turf slopes down to a flat-topped ridge just clear of the highest trees. The path winds down to this ridge, then traverses L into a broad shallow gully leading down into the trees. In 2-2½ hours you come out on a rock-strewn shoulder among scattered Balkan Pines, with a sheepfold among the boulders to your L. This is Petròstrounga *(petròstroonga)* - the stony sheepfold.

From the shoulder you drop down into an open grassy bowl and enter the trees again, where there is a signposted fork in the path. The R branch leads to a spring in 15 minutes. Keep straight on. There is another fork a little further, where you keep straight on again. The R branch leads in 10 minutes to a rock overhang where an eccentric Greek landscape painter, Vassilis Ithakissios, used to live.

Thereafter, the path descends steeply through mixed woods of beech and pine to a little patch of meadow known as Bárba, and thence to the track at *dheeyaklàdhosee*. If you have no car, you will either have to walk down to Litóhoro or hope for a lift.

I strongly recommend going up via refuge A and coming down via Petròstrounga and Diaklàdosi. Though the latter is also a beautiful ascent route, it is long and outside July and August you would have to camp and carry extra provisions. If you are nervous about the Loúki couloir, you will have to make a long detour to get to the summit via Kakì Skàla.

PELION

Map: NSSG 1:200,000 sheet Magnisias

Pelion is a mountainous promontory, not more than 1500 metres high, enclosing the east side of the bay of Vòlos, just north of Èvvia. It is very beautiful and unusually green, especially the seaward eastern slopes, which fall away steeply to the Aegean. Its villages too are remarkably fine and much better preserved than in most other parts of Greece. Local buses from Vòlos (trains and buses from Athens) serve most of them. There are fine sandy beaches too. The few roads are relatively traffic-free and it would be far from unpleasant simply walking on them.

Here, however, are two real hiking routes.

Makrinìtsa to Servìas and Flamoùri monasteries

Walking times: 4¼ and 7½ hours

Makrinìtsa *(makreeneètsa)* is one of the prettiest of the Pelion villages, stepping up the mountainside high above Vòlos. It has hotels and tavernas, and a daily bus service from Vòlos. The central *plateèya* is particularly attractive, with an ancient church shaded by enormous plane trees and a dramatic view over Vòlos and the sea.

Go up the cobbled lane *(kaldereèmee)* behind the church. Branch L at the Pension Sisiliànos and continue up to the top of the village, where you meet a track by a spring and plane tree (10 mins). Turn L up the track. After about 10 minutes (20 mins) a path branches L up the side of the gully on your L. A little way ahead the gully narrows to a trench-like defile, on the upper side of which are some plane trees. Cross the gully by the trees and continue up the L flank. The track remains on the R of the gully. At 42 mins you pass a shrine *(eekòneesma)* on shaly ground right on top of the ridge. The vegetation is nothing but low scrub as far as the eye can see. Continue north up the L side of the ridge, until (55 mins) you reach a small pond on grassy ground just beyond a sheepfold.

Straight ahead (north-east) a gully descends towards fields and orchards on the R flank of a valley. This is the way I went. The true path bears L over the rounded L-hand skyline, i.e. leaving the gully on the R. It is not clear, however, so cast about carefully.

If at a loss, follow me! Straight ahead down the gully. There is a track. At 1 hr 5 mins you pass a spring on the R, then climb up and along through the orchards. At the further end there is an isolated cottage amid gardens on the L below the track, with a considerable canyon beyond. Cut down to the cottage (1 hr 25 mins). Ahead to the L, you can see a track cut into the L flank of the canyon. From the cottage, cut straight downhill. There is no path. You come to the edge of a steep drop, where you can see the track in the canyon bottom. Scramble down into the ravine on your L. Turn R in the streambed and down to the track at 1 hr 55 mins. Turn L and follow the track high along the flank of the canyon until it bends L through a cutting (2 hrs 15 mins). 50 metres beyond the bend, a good path goes R through prickly oak scrub. (The correct path from the pond should hit the track somewhere here, coming down off the slope on the L.)

In a few minutes the path begins to lose height. At 2 hrs 40 mins you hit open grass. 5 minutes later you start to descend into the big valley on your R. It is a rough but excellent path through thick scrub. At 3 hrs 5 mins you cross a bridge in the valley bottom and climb the opposite bank to a crossroads by a spring and large plane tree (3 hrs 15 mins). There is a church on the R. Turn up a track to the R, past two cottages buried in greenery, and take a R fork. You can see the pink roof of the ruined monastery of Servìas *(servèeyas)* in the trees on the slopes ahead of you. Continue up a small gully for a short distance, then cross L and climb up through the woods. Well worn into the forest floor, the path was obviously a major thoroughfare once. At 3 hrs 35 mins you cross a stream by a water pipe. At 4 hrs 10 mins you come to a clearing with poplar trees and a water trough. The ground is well trampled by goats, whose pens are a little higher up the slope. The monastery is a few hundred metres to the L. It was destroyed by a fire accidentally started by a shepherd. Only the church survives. It is a very remote spot. The prudent will stop here -a satisfying destination and a good place to camp.

The path on to Flamoùri is very overgrown and not easy to find. I got lost despite elaborate and accurate directions from the goatherd at Servìas. It is more or less okay as far as a forestry track about 1¼ hours away.

The path starts from the top R corner of the monastery buildings and climbs up through thick oak and beech woods, bearing L. Keep a sharp eye out for the line of the path; it is well disguised by fallen leaves. After 25 minutes you come to a field (4 hrs 35 mins). Keep L along the L edge for a bit, then down to the R (heading just E of N). At 5 hrs you enter a bracken-filled clearing after a short descent. Go up into the woods again and fork L after 50 metres. There are traces of charcoal-burners' activities. The path is very overgrown hereabouts, though the line of it is still plain enough on the ground.

In half an hour (5 hrs 30 mins) you hit a forestry track running along the top of a wooded ridge. Turn L. There is - or was - a path to Flamoúri, to the R about 200 metres along the track by a group of three or four bigger trees. I went down it for half an hour, to the end of a big flat clearing, where, according to the goatherd's instructions, it turned L and I should have been very close to the monastery. As far as I could see, the path disappeared completely ... Try, if you are feeling foolhardy.

The safest thing is to stay on the track, through woodland all the way, for about an hour (6 hrs 30 mins), until you descend to a flat open meadow by an artificial pond and some patches of cultivation. Here another track branches off to the R. Take it - along the R flank of a gully. You reach a fork in 15 minutes (6 hrs 45 mins), where you turn R on a higher track. Where it comes to an end 15 minutes later (7 hrs), a good path sets off into the woods on the L in front of you. Round the head of a gully, past signs of former grandeur -the odd bit of retaining wall - it brings you to the monastery in about 30 minutes (7 hrs 30 mins).

It is a very beautiful place, lost in the middle of nowhere, and now inhabited by only a handful of monks, who live off what they can grow in the monastery garden. The buildings form a semi-fortified square round a courtyard with a much restored 16C church. Rickety stairs and galleries lead to the monks' cells. The monks will put you up, if you are male. A woman is not even allowed to enter the courtyard. Probably they would give her food if she sat meekly at the gate. Orthodox monks are very touchy about dress, for males too (no shorts). Don't upset them. You can't change their ideas, however misguided they may appear to you. And if you antagonise them you may miss the opportunity to savour a wholly medieval way of life. It would be particularly interesting to visit such a place at Easter or the Feast of the Assumption (August 15th), or any major church feast day.

Instead of returning by the same route, go back to the pond at the start of the monastery track and continue R to the village of Kerasiá *(kerasyà)* in about 2½ hours. There are buses to Vólos.

Hània to Zagorà

Walking time: 3 hours

Take any bus from Vólos that goes to the east coast villages via the ski installations, and get off at Hània *(hànya),* where there is a large old-fashioned hotel on the L of the road. Right behind the hotel you will find the beginning of the old cobbled mule road to Zagorà.

The going is all downhill, through woods of stunted beech, with magnificent views of the sea 1000 metres and more below. The path has been cut by the modern road in one or two places and you need to keep a sharp look-out each time for the continuation.

PELOPONNESE

HELMOS (2355m)

Map: NSSG 1:200,000 sheet Achaias

Helmòs lies close to the northern shore of the Peloponnese just south of the Corinth-Patras road. It can be climbed either from Kalàvrita *(kalàvreeta)* - turn-off at Diakòfto - or Sòlos - turn-off at Akràta. Kalàvrita has hotels and a daily bus service from Athens. Sòlos has only an irregular local service.

Sòlos to Mavronèri

Walking time: 5-5½ hours

This is far the best walk on the mountain, through beautiful woods with a varied and gorgeous flora to the dramatic ravine where the 200-metre Mavronèri *(mavronèree)* waterfall gives birth to the river Styx, which, mythology has it, the souls of the dead had to cross in order to enter Hades.

The drive up to Sòlos is pretty spectacular too. A bonus for botanists: the summer-flowering *cyclamen persicum* grows in profusion close to the road higher up.

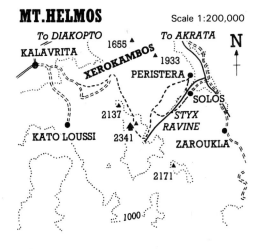

There are two possible routes for the first two hours, one from Sòlos, one from Peristèra, the village on the opposite side of the ravine.

From Sòlos, continue along the track through the village (there is a *magazèe*). A signpost points to the Gòlfos spring. The track follows the L flank of the valley. In 40 minutes you come to a crossroads, signposted: Gòlfos straight on, Kastràki to the R. Turn R in line with the mouth of the Styx ravine, on the opposite side of your valley. The forest presses in closely here. In 10 minutes you reach the river. Cross over. The track continues on the far side. On the L in a clearing is a small white marble pillar commemorating an 1821 battle against the Turks.

Do not go up the track here. Cross the stream coming down the gully on your R. Cross the neck of land dividing this stream from a second one further to the R. Cross the second stream (1 hr) and climb out into a large sloping grassy field. Cross the field diagonally uphill to the top R-hand corner. Unclear in the grass, the path becomes clearer once you enter the trees. The line of the path remains clear, although in places you have to push through encroaching branches. You appear to be, and are, moving away R from the Styx ravine. Don't worry! Cross a water-channel and keep on up. The gradient levels a bit and after about an hour (2 hrs) you reach a T-junction with the well-trodden path from Peristèra. Turn down R for a short distance - the wrong direction for Mavronèri - and you come to a broad gully with a stream, where the woods end. The flat grassy ground on the opposite bank makes a good camp.

This is where you arrive, if you come up by the alternative path from Peristèra. I have only done it going down, when it took 1½ hours all the way to Sòlos. Coming up should take 2-2½ hours.

Coming out of Sòlos, just past the last houses, the track curves round the head of a gully. Take the path which goes R down the L flank of this gully. Cross the river by the bridge at the bottom and climb up to the track in front of you (15 mins). There is a chapel on the L of the track. On the wall of a house on the R, a sign points up to the L, Pros Gounariànika *(goonareeyàneeka)*. Take this path. It leads, past a church on a prominent eminence, to the track again and L to the hamlet of Gounariànika (1 hr 10 mins). From Gounariànika it climbs steadily up the R flank of the valley through the remains of cultivated fields to the edge of the gully mentioned above. Though slightly longer, this is certainly the easier route to find.

160

From the gully, continue up through the forest. After about 55 minutes (say, 3 hrs and 25 mins), you descend to a boulder-strewn streambed with a rocky ravine to the R leading to the foot of a great bare crag. Cross and continue leftward up the opposite bank. At 3 hrs 40 mins you come out on top of a grassy spur. Back into the trees, the path is easy and clear. 15 minutes later you turn a R-hand corner into the mouth of the Styx ravine. A further 5 minutes (4 hrs) brings you to a deep gully where enormous wedges of snow lie late into the spring. The path zigzags up the R side of the gully before crossing. A few paces across a dividing rib of rock, there is a second gully where the path has been eroded and you cross slippery scree.

At 4 hrs 15 mins you come to a wooded spur running down from the crag on the R. The path winds up to a shoulder (4 hrs 20 mins), descends into another gully, winds up to a second shoulder of level rocky ground by some large Black Pines (4 hrs 30 mins) - known as the Hunter's Pass, *to dheeyàselo too keeneegòo*. You look down into the Styx ravine, rising steeply towards the R to Apàno Lithàri, where it begins. The Mavronèri waterfall pours off the cliffs to the R.

To get to it, continue down the path towards the R for another 15 minutes (4 hrs 45 mins), until, below an enormous crag, it peters out - or appeared to, when there was snow on the ground. It may be visible in summer. But, in any case, you can see the waterfall from here.

At your feet is a slippery steep slope of friable rock. I tried to traverse across it, but was driven away from the cliffs by falling rocks. The best thing is to descend to the stream and make your way towards the scree cone running down below the waterfall, where you pick up the path again. It takes about 35 minutes to the foot of the fall (5 hrs 20 mins). In the cave beneath it grows an endemic columbine, *aquilegia amaliae*.

I have not been beyond this point, but a route continues up to the head of the Styx ravine and north or north-west to the HAC refuge (see below) - I should think, not more than 3 hours distant. The highest and third highest peaks of the massif, Psilì Korfì (2355m) and Aetòrahi (2335m), lie south of the Styx ravine. The second highest, Neraidòrahi (2341m), is the one whose crag-foot you have been following all the way up from Peristèra.

Kalàvrita to HAC refuge

Take the road to the war memorial on the hill just outside the town, which commemorates the 1,436 men and boys massacred by the Germans in 1943, and carry on uphill. You come eventually to a large meadow, called Varvoùsi *(varvoòsee)*, where the track crosses a stream bridge. The bald peak of Avgò rises above the valley. From the bridge a path follows the true L bank of the stream, then winds up R through the woods to reach Xeròkambos *(kseròkambos)*, a vast area of flattish pasture at about 1600 metres, in around 2 hours. A forestry track also comes as far as the edge of these pastures - take a sharp L turn some way beyond the Varvoùsi meadow.

From the edge of Xeròkambos, head south, aiming first for the rising ridge opposite (it leads eventually to the Neraidòrahi peak -*nerayeedhòrahee),* then bearing R into the valley below it. On a saddle at the head of this valley you come to the refuge, with a spring below it called *too poolyoò ee vreèsee* - Bird Spring - reached about 2 hours from the head of the track. Neraidòrahi is reached up the ridge to the L of the refuge. For the head of the Styx valley, continue south.

MANI

Map: NSSG 1:200,000 sheet Lakonias

Mani is the Greek name for the promontory that ends in Cape Matapan (Tènaro), the most southerly point of mainland Europe after Cape Tarifa in Spain. It is a rocky, arid region, notorious for its long tradition of internecine feuding. Its villages have the most extraordinary architecture. The houses are tall fortified towers built for defence against the neighbours in these endless vendettas. Today they stand in gaunt and ruined clusters on the hilltops surrounded by palissades of prickly pear cactus. The region is almost wholly depopulated.

There are buses from Yìthion *(yèetheeyo),* south of Sparta, to Areòpolis and Yerolìmena on the west coast. Both places have basic hotels.

Yerolìmena to Tènaro (Cape Matapan)

Walking time: 5 hours

About 10km (2 hours) south of Yerolìmena by the road you come to Vàthia *(vàthya),* the best preserved and most dramatic of the tower villages. EOT has recently converted several of the towers into a hotel, which, to say the least, has somewhat altered the character of the place. There are several shingly beaches close to the road.

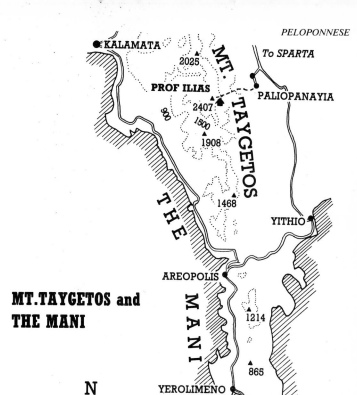

MT.TAYGETOS and THE MANI

N

Scale 1:500,000

The road now continues beyond Vàthia to the narrow isthmus which joins Cape Tenaro to the mainland - about 40 minutes. Cross the isthmus. To the east is an almost circular bay with the tiny hamlet of Pòrto Kàyio on the shore. To the west is Màrmari, a cluster of towers above a beautiful sandy cove.

At the further end of the isthmus go down the valley between the two heights. You pass a small wood on the R and a pretty, green creek on the L. The path runs between dry stone walls, breasts a rise and, after a R fork, descends towards the sea past three or four

163

primitive houses and an incongruous suburban villa on the L. The path follows the shore for a bit, climbs over a couple of intervening spurs, then the cape lighthouse comes into view at the end of a narrow spit of rock (3 hours from Vàthia). It is a wild and lonely spot. If the lighthouse keeper is awake, you will probably be rewarded with an ouzo.

Ahìllio to Korogoniànika and back to Ahìllio

Walking time: 3 hours

Coming from Vàthia (see above), fork L at the start of the isthmus. At the entrance to Ahìllio *(aheèlyo)* (only 3 inhabitants) there is a spring at the foot of a surprisingly lush gully. A path leads from the far side of the village, past a second spring beneath a plane tree, to the beach at the mouth of a dry valley opposite Pòrto Kàyio. Cross the valley and climb to the ridge overlooking the sea (1 hour). Walk up the ridge to the head of the valley on your L. There are some primitive shelters and two abandoned houses on a grassy saddle. At the further end of the saddle, the remains of a *kaldereèmee* lead past an ancient church to the almost deserted village of Korogoniànika, with its gaunt towers lining the hilltop (2 hours). Go down to the track below the village and turn L (R leads to Làyia). Shortly afterwards turn L down a good path descending a gully back to Ahìllio.

PARNONA (1935m)

Map: NSSG 1:200,000 Arkadias

Mt Pàrnona is a long, narrow spine of mountain, running south-east from the Tripoli plateau in the middle of the Peloponnese. It is not a dramatic mountain, but there are beautiful woods and fine views from the summit. Access is via the village of Àyios Pètros, reached either from Àstros on the coast south of the Argos-Tripoli road, or from the Tripoli-Sparta road. There are buses from Tripoli. From Àyios Pètros there is a forest track to the HAC refuge half-way to Vamvakoù *(vamvakoòo)*. It is signposted from the turning outside Àyios Pètros - 14km. There is plenty of room for camping round the refuge, and a spring 5 minutes to the south-east.

Refuge-Krònion peak-track

Walking time: 4½ hours

Set off up the track in front of the refuge and turn L at the first fork.

In 10 minutes you come to a sign on a tree on the L pointing to Krónion. Turn down the path to the L and you hit the track again. Cross, and slightly up to the R, the path continues to descend on the L, through deep bracken. At 15 mins you come to a spring by a grove of walnut trees. A wooded ridge rises opposite and in the distance you can see the summit ridge, with a large cairn of stones on the first peak. Below the walnuts, turn L on the track, and very soon you come to a sign pointing R to Krónion (3 hours). Go down across abandoned terraces through more walnuts into a damp, shady bottom below the wooded ridge, and up to the track on the far side (30 mins). Turn R. Round a L-hand bend and just at the start of a R-hand bend, turn off L up a narrow gully (37 mins). Climb up into a streambed between steep fir-clad slopes. At 50 mins you reach a fork in the streambed. An arrow on a tree points L. Go up the L gully. It is easy going through bracken and grass. The woods become more open. At 1 hr 20 mins you reach a track at the top of the gully. Cross and go up a track opposite. After 40 metres there is a fork. Go up into the trees between the two branches of the fork. The path is not very clear. Gradually leave the gully on your R, moving upwards and slightly L.

After a few minutes in dense forest, you come to a clearing with a steep wooded bank in front of you. Go straight up the bank, still keeping the gully back to your R. Above the trees (1 hr 40 mins) the ground becomes rocky. Head straight up to the ridge above you (1 hr 45 mins) and turn L along the top. In 10 minutes you reach the foot of a steep ascent up the rising ridge line (1 hr 55 mins). There is a sheepfold and some remains of terracing to the east of the ridge.

Climb straight up the ridge to the rounded peak visible ahead (2 hrs 25 mins) - the one marked by the large cairn. 20 minutes further along the ridge you come to Krónion (2 hrs 55 mins). Below to the L is an oval plateau with a little white chapel dedicated to Profîtis Ilías at the northern end. You can see Árgos and Náfplion to the north and the islands of Hýdra and Spétses to the east.

From the summit descend the ridge to the chapel on the edge of the plateau (3 hrs 25 mins). A good path starts behind it and goes down into the trees, keeping R of a gully. At 4 hrs you reach a junction where the path appears to continue L, while straight ahead are the remains of a grassy track. Keep straight ahead. In 3 minutes turn back to the L on a similar track, which brings you up over the bump to the edge of a clearing (4 hrs 2 mins). To the R is an open, level piece of ground. Go straight on in the same direction as before. On your L a steep wooded peak blocks the view of Krónion. Ahead is another wooded ridge. Keep downhill through trees and across clearings. At 4 hrs 12 mins you pass through a small grassy hollow and come, shortly afterwards, to a well-trodden path coming in from the R. Turn L, going downhill towards the foot of the peak blocking your view of the Krónion. The path is wide here with a gully on the R. Ignore a L-hand path at 4 hrs 18 mins and keep straight on. At 4 hrs 20 mins you meet a broad track crossing your line of march at right angles. Turn L down the track, with a sharp drop on your R. At the foot of the peak on your L, the track turns hard R by a stream gully. There is a red arrow on the rocks to the L. Turn down R into the gully. At 4 hrs 35 mins you reach the Áyios Pétros track by a spring. I estimate it to be around 7km from here to Áyios Pétros.

TAYGETOS (2407m)

Map: NSSG 1:200,000 sheet Lakonias

Taygetos *(tayeègetos)* is a long narrow spine of mountain running more or less north-south down the middle of the three prongs of land that terminate the Peloponnese. Access is via Sparta *(spàrtee),* served by frequent buses from Athens (also hitchable). You get a beautiful view of the range as you descend from the hills of Arkadia to the glossy-dark orange groves of the vale of Sparta. The great Byzantine site of Mistra lies in the foothills just west of the town, so don't miss that if you are in the area.

Poliána to Profítis Ilías (2407m)

Walking time: 4½ hours

Stock up with food in Sparta.

There are buses from Sparta as far as the village of Paliopanayià *(palyopanayà),* off the Yíthio road. There, a track, signposted by the HAC, leads west up a long valley to Tòriza and Poliána *(polyana),* nearly 12km. It is a long dusty slog if you have to do it on foot. At Poliána there is a ramshackle house on the R below the track, shaded by two large plane trees, where an old couple spend the summer months. They can provide drinks and a simple meal.

The path to the HAC refuge begins on the L a few minutes further on, by a drunken blue sign pointing into the forest. You come almost immediately to a concrete junction box in a water pipeline. Turn sharp R and five minutes or so later you come to a track. Soon after there is a red HAC arrow on the L. Thereafter there are regular waymarks. Approaching the refuge *(katafeeyo)* you pass the spring of Ayìa Varvàra *(aèeya varvàra)*. It is likely to be dry by late summer, so be prepared.

The refuge - reached after 2½ hours - lies on a broad saddle directly below the conical peak of Profítis Ilías *(profèetees eelèeyas)*. There is plenty of room for camping, and the refuge has a sort of porch which would provide some shelter in bad weather.

The path to the summit starts at the back L corner of the refuge and swings R on a long reach, level and stony at first. Then, leaving the tree-line, it loops up a steep stony bank to a sloping meadow, where it it is marked by wayward, tilting signs, their lettering long obliterated. There is a superb view over Sparta, east to Pàrnona and north to Mènalo. Keep heading R across the slope, towards a distinct secondary peak until, round a steep bend, the path begins to turn back L in the direction of the summit. It slants steadily upward below the ridge, following a natural rock ledge, until, at a distinct gap in the ridge, it turns R and crosses to the far side, whence you look down on the sea in the Gulf of Messenia and northwards into the heart of the range. Turn L and steeply up to the summit in about 25 minutes (4 hrs 30 mins).

There is a squat stone chapel and outbuildings on the summit, used during the celebration of the feast of the Prophet Elijah on July 20th. The view is breathtaking.

ZIRIA (2376m)

Map: NSSG 1:200,000 Korinthias

Zìria *(zèereeya)* is reached via Xylòkastro *(kseelòkastro)* on the Corinth-Patras road and the village of Àno Trìkala, where there is a basic hotel. The drive is superb.

From Àno Trìkala a track winds up on to the central Zìria plateau (2½ hours walk), marked by numerous small hills and gullies. The woods come to an end at the edge of the plateau, which, combined with the absence of any dramatic rock formations, makes Zìria a rather dull climb.

The track continues staight across the plateau, past a cheesemaker's hut and a spring by a low tree. The main refuge is visible on a rise overlooking this hut. There is a second refuge in the ravine across to the L in front of you. The track ends by a group of shepherds' huts at the foot of the bare slope leading to the summit. It is 2 hours direct to the summit from the end of the track, and 3 hours via the second refuge, known as *to speetee too hanyà*.

The redeeming features of the climb are the views of Helmos to the west and the flowers, in particular the endemic *crocus tricolor,* with three horizontal bands of colour in the flower.

ISLAND OF SAMOS
Map: NSSG 1:200,000 sheet Samou

Samos is a beautiful green island with a number of easy walks and an abundant flora, including some Asian species, and creatures like the chameleon, as well as flowers.

Mt. Kerkis (1433m)
Walking time: 4 hours

Start from the hamlet of Votsalàkia on the beach below Marathòkambos and continue a short distance west to a track on the R signposted for the convent of Evangelìstria *evangelèestreeya).*

Walk up the track until, just past a small house, you bear L by a sign saying *pros evangelèestreeyan.* Climb steadily up through the olive groves, winding L-wards along the base of a cliff, until the gradient steepens up to a shoulder with views over the adjacent islands of Fourni and Ikaria. The path zigzags up into pine trees past a ruined hut on the R and neglected-looking terraces. You reach the convent, on the L above the path, after 1½ hours. There is a fountain at the gate.

At the back of the convent, the path climbs up through a pine wood, waymarked by white, then blue crosses on the tree-trunks. At the top, where the trees thin out, the path follows the edge of a steep rocky drop on the R, winding rather vaguely to the top of a rise over-looking the convent wood. Then it continues up a long ridge to the chapel of Profìtis Ilìas (2½ hours). The waymarks are blue crosses painted on the rocks. Past the chapel, on the other side of the ridge, a deep ravine cuts into the mountain, on the further side of which is the summit, Vìgla. Go R-handed into the bottom of the ravine, then L-handed up to Vìgla. It is a dull climb. The view is the thing. Round the summit there grows a lemon-scented herb, in appearance very like thyme, which boiled and sweetened with honey, makes a good herb tea.

Other possibilities

From Kokkåri, just west of the modern town of Samos, a track leads to the 16th century monastery of Vrondiani. Bear L at a fork shortly after the start of the track. After the first 25 minutes keep a look-out for the old footpath, on the R, which leads to the monastery in just over an hour. Continuing on beyond the monastery, to the end of the track, you come to a spring by some apple orchards, where the now rare red peony *mascula* blooms in spring. From there you can climb the Lazaros peak in front of you (about 1 hour's climb).

If you branch R at the fork just out of Kokkåri, it leads you to the path to the village of Vourliôtes (1½ hours), whence another path leads west to Manolåtes in a further 1½ hours.

Another good walk is to the beach of Åyia Paraskevî on the north shore of the island, behind the town of Samos. The path starts by the football ground at the back of the town.

PART FOUR

Glossary

Here are a number of Greek terms commonly encountered when you walk in the mountains. If you do not speak Greek, you are going to hear people saying them to you rather than the other way round. For this reason, I have arranged them in simple categories with the Greek first. If the spelling looks funny it is because I have tried to find combinations of English letters which, if pronounced in the normal English way, will produce sounds as near as possible to the Greek. It is basically the system used by the Collins Contemporary Greek Dictionary. The dots show which syllable you should stress - stress them hard!

a is pronounced as it is in *hat, e* as in *get, o* as in *hot, ee* as in *feet, oo* as in *food*. *g* is always hard, as in *goat*. *h* sounds like the *ch* in Scottish *loch*. *dh* sounds like *th* in *then*. *r* is rolled and *s* is always as in *soft*.

Terrain/Landmarks

aneefóra	ascent
apótomos	steep, precipitous
dhásos	wood, forest
dheemósyo	road, track
dhéndro	tree
dheeyakládhosee	fork, junction
dheeyáselo	saddle, col
dheeyastàvrosee	crossroads
dhrómos	road (sometimes refers to path)
eedhragoyèeo	water channel, pipeline
èepsoma	height, knoll, bump
èesyoma	level ground
ekleesèeya	church, chapel
èlata	fir trees
faràngee	ravine, gorge
gremós	cliff, precipice
haràdhra	ravine, gorge
homatòdhromos	dirt road
horàfee	field, cultivated path
horyò	village
kalderèemee	cobbled mule path
kalèeva	hut
katafèeyo	mountain refuge
kateefóra	descent
katseekòdhromos	goat path, i.e. not a proper path
keelàdha	valley

170

kolónes	telegraph poles
konákya	shepherds' huts
kordhéles	zigzags, in path or road
koreefogramèe	summit ridge, peak line
korfeé	summit, peak
làka	grassy clearing or hollow, cwm
langkàdhee	gully, espy. wooded
leémnee	lake, tarn
leevàdhee	meadow, alpage
lófos	hill
loókee	couloir
loótsa	pond, tarn
magazèe	village shop, cafe
magazèes	keeper of above
mandrèe	sheepfold
meélos	mill
monastèeree	monastery
monopàtee	path
orthoplayà	vertical cliff
oxyà	beech tree
paralèeya	seashore
peegàdhee	well
peenakeèdha	signpost
peeyeé	spring (of water)
péfka	pine trees
pétra	stone
platànee	plane tree
playá	slope, hillside
poornárya	prickly oak scrub
potàmee	river
potamyà	riverbed
pròpodhes	foothills
ràhee	ridge
reéza	foot of slope or cliff
réma	stream
rematyà	streambed, gully
sàra	scree
skoléeyo	school
smeéksee	confluence of streams
speelyà	cave
speétee	house
stànee	sheepfold
stroónga	sheepfold
tabèla	signpost
teéhos	wall
thàlasa	sea

tsombànees	shepherd
velaneedyà	oak tree
voonò	mountain
vràhos/vràhya	rock(s)
vreèsee	spring (of water)
yeemnòs	bare, treeless
yèfeera	bridge

Directions

apènandee	opposite
ap'aftèe tee meryà	on this side
apò teen àlee meryà	on the other side
areesterà	on the left
dheèpla	next to
dheksyà	on the right
edhò	here
eèsya	straight ahead
eèsya kato	straight down
eèsya pano	straight up
ekèe	there
hameelà	low down
kat'eftheèya	straight ahead
kàto	down
kondà	near
makreeyà	far
mèhree	up to, as far as, until
pàno	up
pèra	over there, beyond
pròs	towards
pseelà	high up
anevènees...	you go up...
katevènees...	you go down...
pas...	you go...
pernàs...	you cross/pass...
mòlees peràsees...	as soon as you have crossed/passed...
parakalò, o dhròmos ya...?	can you tell me the way to...?
parakalò, to monopàtee ya...?	can you show me the path to...?
pòses òres èene?	how many hours is it?

Weather

astrapèe	lightning	hyònee	snow	seènefa	clouds
aèras	wind	kateyeèdha	storm	vrohèe	rain
eèlyos	sun	kreèyo	cold	zèstee	hot
feesàyee	it's windy	omeèhlee	mist		

172

Transport

aftokeèneeto	car, vehicle
forteegó	lorry
leoforéeyo	bus
tee óra févyee	what time does it leave?
tee òra ftànee	what time does it arrive?
boreètee na me pàrete?	can you take me?

Eating and shopping

avgà	eggs
batereèya	battery
elyès	olives
faeè	food
gàla	milk
gàzee	gas
heelòpeeta	kind of rural pasta
konsèrves	tinned food
nerò	water
psomèe	bread
venzeènee	petrol
speèrta	matches

Sleeping and camping

dhomàtyo	room
kameenéto	camping stove
krevàtee	bed
ksenodhoheèyo	hotel
ksenònas	guesthouse
skeenèe	tent
borò na steèso tee skeenèe?	can I put my tent up?

Numbers

èna/mèeya	one (masc/feminine)	èekosee	twenty
dheèyo	two	treeyànda	thirty
trèes/trèeya	three	sarànda	forty
tèseres/tèsera	four	penèenda	fifty
pènde	five	ekseèna	sixty
èksee	six	evdhomeènda	seventy
eftà	seven	ogdhònda	eighty
oktò	eight	eneneènda	ninety
enyà	nine	ekatò	one hundred
dhèka	ten	dheeyakòsya	two hundred
èndheka	eleven	pendakòsya	five hundred
dhòdheka	twelve	heèlya	one thousand
dhekatrèes	thirteen	dhèeyo heelyàdhes	two thousand
dhekatesères	fourteen		
dhekapènde	fifteen		

Time

pènde leftà	five minutes
èna tètarto	quarter of an hour
meesèe òra	half an hour
mèeya òra	one hour
meeyàmeesee òres	one and a half hours
dhèeyo òres	two hours
stees mèeya	at 1 o'clock
stees trèeya ke tètarto	at quarter past three
stees tèseres pàra pende	at five to four
apòyevma	afternoon
àvreeyo	tomorrow
hthès	yesterday
mèra	day, daytime
neèhta	night, nightime
proèe	morning
seèmera	today
vràdhee	evening

Animals

arkoòdha	bear	moolàree	mule
ayetòs	eagle	pròvata	sheep
feèdhee	snake	skeelyà	dogs
katseèkya	goats	zòa	mules
leèkos	wolf		

Miscellaneous

ne	yes
òhee	no
leègo	a little
polèe	a lot, very
parakalò	please
efhareestò	thank you
meekrò	small
megàlo	big
kalò	good
kakò	bad
kaleemèra	good day
yàsoo/yàsas	good health to you (sing/plural)
tee kànees	how are you?
poso kànee?	how much is it?

PRINTED BY CARNMOR PRINT AND DESIGN
95/97 LONDON ROAD, PRESTON, LANCASHIRE

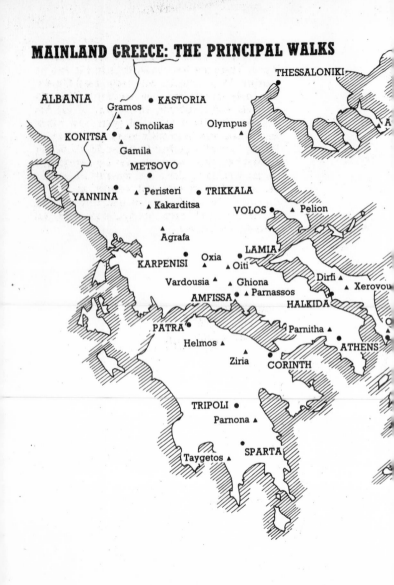

MAINLAND GREECE: THE PRINCIPAL WALKS

ALBANIA

THESSALONIKI

● KASTORIA

Gramos ▲

▲ Smolikas

Olympus ▲

KONITSA ●

▲ Gamila

METSOVO ●

YANNINA ●

▲ Peristeri   ● TRIKKALA

▲ Kakarditsa

VOLOS ●   ▲ Pelion

▲ Agrafa

Oxia ●   LAMIA ●

KARPENISI ●   ● Oiti

Vardousia ▲   ▲ Ghiona   Dirfi ▲   ▲ Xerovou

AMFISSA ▲   ▲ Parnassos

HALKIDA

PATRA ●   Parnitha ▲

Helmos ▲   ATHENS ●

Ziria ▲

CORINTH

TRIPOLI ●

Parnona ▲

Taygetos ▲   SPARTA ●